M000120404

JOINT FORCE
LEADERSHIP

HOW SEALS AND FIGHTER PILOTS
LEAD TO SUCCESS

JIM "BOOTS" DEMAREST | Air Force Fighter Pilot
MARK MCGINNIS | Navy SEAL

A POST HILL PRESS BOOK
An Imprint of Post Hill Press
ISBN: 978-1-64293-483-0
ISBN (eBook): 978-1-64293-484-7

Joint Force Leadership:
How SEALs and Fighter Pilots Lead to Success

Interior design and composition by Sarah Heneghan,
sarah-heneghan.com

Post Hill Press
New York • Nashville
posthillpress.com

Published in the United States of America

TABLE OF CONTENTS

PART ONE: FOCUS

PART TWO: TRUST

PART THREE: COMMUNICATION

PREFACE

Leadership is about people, pure and simple. It involves having the right people in the right place doing the right thing at the right time. It is hard work, requiring constant effort sustained over long periods—and it is not easy. There are some who say leaders are born. Yet while we are indeed born with the skills needed to lead, we prove, time and again, that leadership can be taught and learned. And nowhere is this more evident than in our nation's military.

We are both products of some of the best leadership laboratories anywhere: United States military service academies. As cadets and midshipmen, we studied civilian and military leadership in great detail. More importantly, we have put that study to work "out in the real world" and have honed our skills in the crucible of combat and through battles in the boardroom. Our lifetime of military and civilian leadership experience has taught us lessons we feel compelled to share. Our intent here is to provide simple, practical, time- and battle-tested tools you can use right now to improve your leadership skills.

We chose *Joint Force Leadership* as the title of our book because we wanted to highlight the need for people with different experiences to unite behind a common goal. In military parlance, a "Joint Force" is the combination of forces from different service branches into a single unit. Each comes with its own culture, identity, and vocabulary. And just like corporate teams, getting these diverse groups to work together creates a unique problem set, and leading these teams is varsity-level work.

Plenty of ink has already been spilled over the science of leadership. And so, rather than taking a purely academic approach, we will share a framework for leadership. We will also share the stories and lessons learned by us, and those we've worked with and for, in an effort to make these leadership concepts come alive and show how you can apply them to your own life.

If you focus on our framework, trust in the fact we can all learn something new about leadership, and believe, as we do, that communication is the linchpin of leadership, we are certain this book will help you navigate the challenges and opportunities of your lifelong leadership journey.

Commander Mark McGinnis
United States Navy
SEAL

Colonel Jim "Boots" Demarest
United States Air Force
Fighter Pilot

ABOUT THE AUTHORS

The stories which follow are designed to drive home our leadership model of focus, trust, and communication. Mark's SEAL stories are denoted with the Navy SEAL Trident while Boots' fighter pilot stories are marked with pilot wings to make it easier for the reader to identify who is telling the story. To better understand our perspectives, it might help to know a little more about us.

Mark McGinnis is a graduate of the U.S. Naval Academy and four-year varsity football player with twenty-four years of Special Operations experience as a Navy SEAL. As a SEAL, Mark held leadership positions at all levels of command and has led SEAL missions worldwide. Following his active-duty service, Mark worked for a Fortune 500 medical devices company as a frontline sales representative and regional sales director. He is the founder and managing director of the SEAL Legacy Foundation, a nonprofit providing direct support to the families of fallen SEALs.

Jim "Boots" Demarest is a graduate of the U.S. Air Force Academy with over twenty years of military experience and currently serves in the Florida Air National Guard. He spent ten years as an active-duty F-15 fighter pilot, was a distinguished graduate of the Air Force Fighter Weapons School "Top Gun" program, and served in Operation Desert Storm. Following his active-duty service, Boots graduated from Cornell Law School, where he served as managing editor of the *Cornell Law Review*. He then spent nine years as a commercial litigation attorney in a national law firm before entering the professional speaking and consulting world in 2002.

Together, Mark and Boots are the founders of Joint Force Leadership, a full-service leadership and consulting company.

INTRODUCTION

The view from the surface is different than the view from the air. Our dilemma is to appreciate and reconcile these differences when we team up to accomplish a mutual goal. Nowhere is this dilemma more evident than when comparing SEALs to fighter pilots. For the sake of simplification, we will offer general observations to make our point, understanding that any time we generalize, it is easy to find exceptions.

We tend to think of air power as a strategic asset, somewhat limited in scope and duration but available over a large area to create wide-ranging effects. SEALs and ground forces, on the other hand, have a more tactical focus, although they often bring effects of strategic significance. Just ask Osama bin Laden or the Somali pirates who kidnapped Captain Phillips of the cargo ship *Maersk Alabama*.

Culture for ground forces tends to be more structured, while pilot culture tends to be more fluid.

INTRODUCTION

Leadership in airpower is developed deliberately, while leadership on the ground is hyper-accelerated. Ground teams boast a collective accountability, while air power focuses more on individual accountability. Finally, ground forces tend to communicate horizontally, at the line of sight, while air power necessarily communicates over a more vertically developed network.

Our point here is simple: we have vastly different perspectives, yet we regularly come together to execute complex, no-fail missions, and our results speak for themselves. The key to successful missions, whether conducted on land or water, is leadership, plain and simple. And the same holds true in business when teams collaborate on any project, especially when the teams are made up of people with highly specialized yet divergent skill sets. However, this all starts with focus.

OUR DILEMMA

Ground Power	Versus	Air Power
TACTICAL	*Perspective*	STRATEGIC
STRUCTURED	*Culture*	FLUID
ACCELERATED	*Leadership*	DELIBERATE
COLLECTIVE	*Accountability*	INDIVIDUAL
HORIZONTAL	*Communication*	VERTICAL

PART ONE

FOCUS

Be the Master of Right Now

—U.S. Navy SEAL leadership principle

CHAPTER 1

HAPPY BIRTHDAY

Saturday night. I'm at home in Coronado, California, surrounded by friends, about to blow out the candles on my birthday cake when I get a call from the command.

My Platoon was recalled to conduct a rescue of an American citizen who was on his private yacht. The only other passenger on board, his eleven-year-old grandson, had managed to radio the Coast Guard for help. Unfortunately, their choppers were out of range. It was up to us.

As a young Lieutenant just days into commanding my first Navy SEAL platoon, I was appointed leader for this H. A. op (humanitarian assistance operation). Within minutes, my team was assembled, and within

3

an hour, we were aboard an Air Force transport headed for the Pacific.

The world of a SEAL moves fast. Constant change and challenging environments are the spaces we thrive in. As a young Lieutenant with little "real world" experience, to say that I needed a leadership framework to help guide my decision making is the understatement of understatements. Fortunately for the yacht owner and my team, SEAL training taught me everything I needed.

Thirty-six hours later, I was back home finally getting to dig into that birthday cake. I'd just turned twenty-seven years old.

CHAPTER TWO

ZULU ALERT

Bitburg Air Base in Germany was a "go to war" environment in the 1980s. The base hosted the 36th Tactical Fighter Wing, which was equipped with three combat-coded F-15C squadrons. Cold War tensions ran high in Europe during this time, and Bitburg was center stage. Seventy-five percent of our dedicated air-to-air fighter aircraft were housed in hardened shelters littering the base, and every three months we conducted major exercises preparing for World War III. As a young Lieutenant, my first job was to become a mission-ready pilot, fully qualified to fly any mission required, and my single focus was on being ready to fly, fight, and win. Nothing else mattered.

Our "go to war" mentality was supported by action. Four fully combat-loaded F-15 Eagles sat on Zulu alert, a 24/7/365 quick-reaction force where pilots and crew chiefs sat ready to scramble against any threat. When the horn went off, we had to be airborne in five minutes, day or night, good weather or bad. By late 1985, I was a mission-ready flight lead sitting alert every couple of weeks, honed and razor-sharp.

"Three Six, Copper Ring," crackled over the squawk box. Go time. I raced for the pole as the claxon sounded, sliding down a floor to the alert bay where my Eagle lay waiting. I scampered up the ladder, crew chief in tow, stepped on the ejection seat, and reached over to activate the jet fuel starter (JFS) before sitting down. As the JFS spun up, I slid into my harness with the help of my crew chief. As the crew chief raced down the ladder, I donned my helmet and cranked the right motor.

As the motor spun up, the hydraulic system came to life and the flight controls shuttered to the ready position. The generator quickly came online, and the cockpit lit up. I raced through the scramble checklist and checked in the flight. "Lima Alpha Zero One ready for words," I called.

I read back the words and signaled my crew chief to pull chocks. Chocks out, I rolled out of the barn, through the gates, and down the high-speed taxiway toward the departure end of the runway. "Four minutes," called the command post, letting me know that four minutes had passed since the alarm had sounded. I had less than sixty seconds to get airborne. I looked over my shoulder to see my wingman taxiing out behind me. We were good. I made the turn onto the active runway, slammed the throttles forward to full afterburner, and, just fifteen hundred feet later, lifted off into the German sky, ready for whatever action lay ahead.

★ ★ ★ ★ ★

FOCUS STARTS BY TARGETING MISSION SUCCESS WITH SPECIFIC GOALS

Our leadership journeys started in different places and took very different paths, yet in many ways our destinations have been the same—we have led military and civilian teams through incredible challenges and consistently delivered results.

We have taken our teams into harm's way and returned intact after every mission. Between the two of us, we have completed four hundred SEAL missions and fourteen hundred fighter sorties and brought our teams home after every single one. We have, of course, suffered bumps and bruises along the way, and haven't always enjoyed complete victory, yet we have enjoyed sustained excellence over time by being the master of right now. Step one of focus is to attack challenges with specific goals.

CHAPTER 3

MERIDIAN GOLD

Meridian Gold was a midsize gold-producing company headquartered in Reno, Nevada, with worldwide operations focused in South America. The company was small, about 350 employees, captained by a seven-person leadership team headed by CEO Brian Kennedy. Brian was a 1965 graduate of the Naval Academy determined to grow the company. When I started my work with the company in 2003, Meridian was producing about 350,000 ounces of gold per year. Brian's goal was to get to one million ounces a year, but he knew he needed complete buy-in from the team to reach that milestone.

Brian started by gathering his leaders from around the world for a round of strategic planning. He knew that his goal was attainable but was equally sure that, unless the entire team bought into the goal, it was just a dream. Our strategic planning work began with a hard look at the internal environment at Meridian Gold and the external environment of the global gold mining industry. Next was the challenge of getting his team to think beyond what they thought they could do and "discover" that they could take the company a lot further.

After a few months of strategic planning, his team had created a vision. Instead of drafting a long document that nobody would ever read, they elected to simply draw a picture. Meridian's picture was of a mountain. On the slopes were the major milestones the team would have to hit along their way to the top, and at the summit was a flag that bore the number 1,000,000. Meridian's mountain was posted everywhere. It was prominently displayed at the company's headquarters in Reno, at its major mining operation in Chile, and at any place they did business. It was their mountain and became the focus of all their energy.

Just three years after I finished my work with Meridian, they were bought out by Yamana Gold, and all my C-level friends were rewarded with, quite appropriately, very nice golden parachutes.[1]

---

[1] Laura Mandaro, "Meridian agrees to Yamana's $3.5 billion merger bid," MarketWatch, Sept. 24, 2007, https://www.marketwatch.com/story/yamana-meridian-forge-35-billion-gold-merger

CHAPTER 4

HELL WEEK

SEALs learn plenty about goal setting during Hell Week. Hell Week starts on a Sunday, but you don't know what time it's going to start. It ends on a Friday, but you don't know what time it's going to end. It is 127 hours long with four hours of sleep—not four hours a night but four hours *total*. Ambient air temperatures during the day average 70 degrees in San Diego, dropping into the high 40s to low 50s at night. The water temperature is a steady 55 degrees, so you are cold all the time. Your body shakes uncontrollably as you can't generate enough heat. You're chafed everywhere, with open and oozing sores, including on top of your head from carrying around your boat everywhere you go.

You can't pick up your neck from the weight of the boat bouncing on your head.

When you start Hell Week, the idea is, "I want to make it to Friday." But what you learn pretty quickly, starting on Sunday night, is that "I just want to make it to Monday." And then you make it to Monday and start thinking, "I want to make it to Tuesday." And then what happens is you start realizing that you need smaller goals that you can accomplish faster to keep you moving forward. And then as you wear down, more and more, you just want to make it from breakfast to lunch. "If I can make it to lunch, I want to make it to dinner." And then it goes even further down to, "I just want to make it through this evolution. I'll deal with the next one when it comes. If I could just make it through this evolution, then I can push the reset button and make it to the next one." And then the last twenty-four hours, it simply becomes, "If I make it through this hour, then I can work on the next hour."

So you start with this broad goal of making it through Hell Week and putting on that brown T-shirt, and it devolves into "I want to make it through this next hour." And while there's no such thing as Hell Week in a business setting, the idea of breaking down a larger goal into smaller, seemingly more manageable goals in order to meet the main objective is equally applicable. When we work with businesses, we ask:

"What is your overarching goal? What are you trying to accomplish?" Once that question has been answered, it's about building a pathway or roadmap that has milestones or intermediate mile markers. These give your people a sense of accomplishment, and also help you track progress toward the ultimate goal, whatever it is. If you can establish smaller steps that lead you to a long-range destination, it's easier for your people to stay on the path. They don't get lost because they have a map with checkpoints along the way, and before they know it, they've reached the end destination, rather than getting lost chasing a yearlong goal.

CHAPTER 5

SMARTS GOALS

Simply setting smaller goals isn't enough on its own. We have often said that a plan without goals is a wish. But we need to go further than that. For goals to help steer your team to success, they must be clear. We subscribe to SMARTS goals, and no, that is not a misprint. Most people know of SMART goals, namely Specific, Measurable, Achievable, Realistic, and Time-bound, but in our view, following that guideline is not enough. Goals must first be *Strategic*. They must directly align with the long-term vision established for your organization so that your team can draw a straight line from the goal to the desired end state. If they cannot, the logical next question is, "Why are we about to expend resources to go after this?"

Unfortunately, all too often, we hear the response, "Because we've always done it that way." This is a red flag. If you ever hear that answer, dig deeper. And if you find a compelling, strategic reason, continue. If not, you will do your team a big favor by giving them back the time they would have spent chasing down a task that fails to move the needle enough to justify the effort.

Once we have a strategically aligned goal, it must then be measurable, achievable, realistic, time-bound, and specific. A few thoughts here.

Measurement is critical, but be careful what you measure because what you measure will drive behavior. We cannot count the number of times we've seen a sales manager set a gross sales number and omit any mention of margin. Without the right limits, the sales team could race out the door and discount to hit the number while killing the P&L.

Achievable means believable, not easy. Stretch goals are great if we call them what they are. But it is imperative that, even with stretch goals, you and your team both believe the goal is achievable; otherwise, people will give it lip service and will lack the commitment required to meet or exceed the challenge.

Realistic is in the eyes of the beholder. Often, as a leader, you are privy to information not known to the rest of your team. Sometimes it is information you simply cannot share. More often, it is information you can and should share to improve team buy-in to the goals.

Time-bound sounds easy but is often the most difficult to adhere to. Time is the most valuable resource you have, and the same is true for every member of your team. Putting a date on the calendar takes no effort. Living up to that date is another matter altogether.

Specific assumes that everyone who reads the goal has a collective understanding of the terms used. Sometimes this is true; other times, not so much. In our experience, one thing is sure: few will step up and ask the meaning of a goal in front of a group of people, so be careful assuming that everyone understands your terms and acronyms.

Once we get the goals tightened up, it is time to show we care more about our people than ourselves, and band together to place the needs of the team ahead of those of the individual.

★ ★ ★ ★ ★

PUT TEAM FIRST AND OTHERS ABOVE SELF

We believe wholeheartedly in the saying, "Put team above self, and care for others more than you do yourself." These are the hallmarks of leadership. You must show that the good of the team comes first, and that the success of others matters more than your success. It is easy to do these things when everything is going well. The challenge for a leader is to stick to this principle when the going gets tough, or for a SEAL, when it really gets tough.

CHAPTER 6

CLASS LEADER

S EALs are elite not just because they are called upon
for the toughest missions under "No Fail" situations,
but also because of their training exercises, which are
the most challenging in the world. Indeed, many are
called but few are chosen. The attrition rate during the
twenty-six-week Basic Underwater Demolition/SEAL
(BUD/S) training challenge is over 80 percent.

Training to become a SEAL taught me some of the
most important leadership lessons of my life, and I was
immediately thrust into a leadership role when I was
selected as Class Leader for BUD/S Class 211. It was
not an opportunity I sought out. Truth be told, selection as Class Leader was based purely on date of rank.
Simply put, I was the oldest Naval Academy graduate

with the highest class standing. As I would soon find out, it's not exactly a good thing to be the Class Leader.

For SEALS, deliberate care is of the utmost importance. A dirty weapon or loose boot could cost you time or even your life. That's why we have official standards for things as seemingly minor as how to tie your boots (laces under, tied in a square knot). And in a large group, someone is guaranteed to screw this up, and when they do, they don't get in trouble—the Class Leader does. Every mistake a follower makes is *your* mistake. The insane pressures and responsibilities of being the BUD/S Class Leader made it a total leadership accelerant, especially as Hell Week approached.

Hell Week is 127 hours of, well, hell. As Class Leader, I was responsible for everything—and part of that was to lead. In the afternoon leading up to the start of Hell Week, the instructors moved us to the beach and set us up in big green GP (general purpose) tents. I was leading my team through this event when the instructors yelled, "BREAK OUT!" Every single instructor exploded onto the beach spraying fire hoses, shooting blank machine guns, throwing grenade simulators, and yelling through bullhorns to roust us from the tents. They were breaking us in by creating a "fog of war" environment during the first few hours. It was mad chaos as guys ran around struggling to get into position for drills.

As Class Leader, I had to keep some semblance of order, which was not easy. Every few minutes, the instructors would yell at me to get a "muster," and I'd have to organize my men for inspection. It was nonstop and relentless, and it only got worse from there.

Hell Week's hardest evolution is Monday night's Steel Piers. It might be the most grueling thing we did. We were taken down to the boat basin and ordered to tread water while still in uniform. Since we had a winter Hell Week, the water was unbelievably frigid from the currents coming into San Diego from the north. As Class Leader, I, along with the class LPO (senior enlisted man), had to get our class perfectly aligned, like synchronized swimmers. And we had to do that without speaking a single word.

The task is not the point, though. Taking your mind and body to the absolute limits is. Nearby, a doctor with a stopwatch takes your body right to exposure limits. At that point, the instructors get you out of the water, lay you down on steel piers, and spray you with freezing cold water while you do push-ups. Once you've warmed up a bit, you take off your shirt and get back into the water. Get up to the exposure limit again, get back out of the water, exercise on the steel piers, take off your pants, and jump back in the water. Rinse and repeat. It's like strip poker with a new piece of clothing coming off every time. The mental anguish is extraordinary.

The single most valuable leadership lesson I learned during Hell Week was that if you keep your focus on the end goal (in our case, the Trident), you will succeed. But, if you focus more on short-term pleasures—which in the case of Hell Week might simply be a cup of coffee and a warm blanket—you will fail and eventually quit. If I thought Steel Piers was bad, as Hell Week progressed, I discovered it just got more and more grueling.

Instructors work in shifts, and the ones who come on after midnight are nicknamed "the Princes of Darkness." They're always the hardest instructors with the worst reputations. They'll make you do things like run along the beach for three miles with a boat on your head before forcing you to stop and bury it in the sand using only your paddles to dig. Or surf torture, which has you lying in pounding waves at arm's length from your fellow men, nearly drowning as you sing historical BUD/S songs. They get a kick out of that one.

By Wednesday night, you've entered a zombie state. Physically, you're completely broken. You've become permanently stooped over, like some old guy in a nursing home. You can barely lift your neck up, and, just when you think you can't take another step or breathe another breath, you get your first chance to sleep. That's the worst time of the entire week.

You're given four hours of sleep during Hell Week. Four total hours. Those are the worst four hours of your entire life because you're freezing so badly.

The smells of Hell Week are shocking, like raw sewage. The sights are even more disgusting. Oozing holes explode over everyone's body from constant chafing. The top of your head has had a boat on it all week, and so much skin has scraped away that it feels like your brain is peeking out. Physically, you're a mess. But that's the point of Hell Week. There is no other military training in the world quite like BUD/S. It is literally designed to make you *want* to quit.

Wednesday night of Hell Week was actually a bit of a break compared to the agony we'd gone through the previous three days. You might not consider it a "break," but at that point, we sure did. This little break consisted of a few hours of swim races in the pool. The only reason these races weren't completely meaning- less was because the winner of each race was rewarded with one minute in a hot shower. A single minute might not sound like much, but believe me, it's an absolute luxury after freezing all week.

Now this should come as no surprise, but SEALs are literally *the* most competitive people on the planet. If there are two SEALs in a room, it usually only takes a few minutes for a competition to spring up. Ping-Pong, shooting pool, even just some good old-fashioned arm wrestling, we can't help but challenge each other and always try to beat each other at something. For the kind of men who dream of being SEALs, it's simply our nature.

So, as you can imagine, during Hell Week, with everyone trying to impress the instructors—and something as coveted as a hot shower on the line—these races were straight-up *heated*. They had been going on steadily for an hour when our BUD/S instructor decided to throw a little wrench into our fun and give me my first crucial test as our Class Leader.

"Mr. McGinnis, what would *you* do to get your men *ten* straight minutes in the hot shower?"

Wow, what a question! Without flinching, though, I knew the only answer I could possibly give. "Sir, if you put my men in the hot shower for ten minutes, I'll stand by myself in the cold shower the *entire* time."

The instructor nodded thoughtfully, I guess he was impressed. Impressed enough to quickly accept my offer.

My men were hooting and hollering as they hopped out of the chilly pool, wearing just Speedos, and got under the hot shower. Meanwhile, I took my lumps and headed for the cold one right beside it. As the showers both turned on, I watched my men, my fellow brothers in arms, luxuriating under the thick steam. All the pain and frigidness of the past three days were being washed away, along with their goose-bumped pores, cleansing their addled minds and reviving their weary bodies. At the same time, under that forty-degree fire hose of cold water, I could barely keep my eyes open and hardly stop my teeth from chattering.

I was focusing as hard as I could, just wanting to get through that seemingly endless ten minutes so I could truly live up to my end of the bargain when I noticed something: my men had stopped enjoying that glorious hot shower. In fact, they were now staring at me, watching me struggling to stand, clearly concerned as they observed my intense pain.

Without a word, and after just thirty total seconds, all my men left their hot shower together to join me in my cold one. As I was stone-cold frozen by now, they huddled around me with their now-warm bodies, trying to bring my arctic body temperature up to theirs. Amazingly, it actually started to work, and my pain began to subside. Even more amazingly, at that exact moment, our instructor turned off the cold water.

The BUD/S instructor was so inspired by my team's utter selflessness, so impressed by their empathy toward me, that he decided to let us *all* take a ten-minute hot shower as a reward. We had unwittingly demonstrated one of the major tenets of leadership: care for others more than you care for yourself.

CHAPTER 7

TEAM OVER SELF

The ethos of team over self has carried over to our work with professional sports teams. Coach Tom Coughlin is one of the most successful coaches in National Football League history. His first NFL head coaching job was with the Jacksonville Jaguars when they entered the league in 1995 as an expansion team. They made the playoffs in four of the team's first five years, including two trips to the AFC Championship game. Later he would coach the New York Giants to two Super Bowl victories, and over his coaching career would amass over 180 regular and postseason wins.[2] We were first introduced to him while working with the New York Giants.

---

2   Tom Coughlin, *Earn the Right to Win* (New York: Portfolio/ Penguin, 2013).

Coach Coughlin is an energetic and passionate football coach. He loves the game, the players, and the thrill of competition. But the one quality that sticks out above the rest is his relentless (almost maniacal) emphasis on team over everything else. The walls of the New York Giants' training facility are lined with quotes about teamwork, like this:

BIG BLUE WARRIOR CREED
KEEP YOUR EYE ON THE PRIZE
NO CHALLENGE TOO DIFFICULT
NO SACRIFICE OR SELF-DENIAL TOO GREAT
TEAM FIRST!

Before every game he would craft a unique pep talk, which included his thoughts, points of emphasis, quotes, and themes. But the one thing that would make it into every single talk was the idea of team, and he would reinforce this message during and after the game. Coach believes, as we do, that when you put team over self, you can accomplish so much more together than any one person can alone.

CHAPTER 8

NEVER LEAVE YOUR WINGMAN

Life as a fighter pilot when the movie *Top Gun* came out was good. No, it was great. While the movie represents Hollywood's take on fighter pilots, there are a couple of things the movie gets right, and one of them comes from the quote "You never, never leave your wingman."[3]

While initial flight training emphasizes the skills needed to fly and fight in an airplane, in fighters, we quickly evolve toward working together, and our basic fighting element is a two-ship. Each two-ship has one

---

3   Tom Cruise, *Top Gun*, directed by Tony Scott (Hollywood: Paramount Pictures, 1986).

designated flight lead and one designated wingman, but don't confuse role with experience. While generally the more experienced pilot serves as flight lead, this is not always the case. Sometimes our most senior pilots fly as wingmen, just like in business when a more senior person serves in a supporting role. The key to the relationship between flight lead and wingman lies in clearly defined roles and responsibilities

The flight lead has overall responsibility for employing the two-ship in accordance with the plan and stated objectives for the mission. The wingman supports the flight lead and stands ready to step in and lead if needed. This relationship starts in the planning phase and lasts until the mission and post-flight debrief is completed, both in combat and in training.

We train like we fight, so here is what a two-ship, air-to-air training mission might look like. We brief, step to the jets, start, taxi, and take off together, following a precise timeline. Once airborne, the flight lead and wingman have specific duties. On departure, the flight lead is navigating to the training area, talking on the radio, and directing system checks. The wingman is flying in the prescribed formation position, backing up the navigation, and listening to the radios. Simultaneously, each pilot is monitoring their aircraft systems, fuel, and weapons status.

NEVER LEAVE YOUR WINGMAN

Entering the training airspace, the formation changes to the pre-briefed tactical spread and accelerates to tactical speeds, usually in the 450- to 500-knot range, but often faster. During ingress, each of us has an area of responsibility to monitor via radar, and the engagement starts when the "bad guys" cross into our defended airspace. The flight lead decides when to commit to an intercept and what tactics to employ, while the wingman stays in formation and works the radar.

Once we merge with our adversaries, our tactics become more defensive. We scan the skies for bogeys and bandits while checking our six o'clock, that area directly behind our aircraft where we are most vulnerable to attack. The problem is we cannot see our most vulnerable spot, the area directly behind and below our aircraft. That's where you've got to trust your wingman—literally with your life. We check each other's six o'clock, ready for a defensive break turn at the first sign of trouble. And we will stay and fight together until both of us or neither of us comes home. We know no other way. Never, never leave your wingman.

★ ★ ★ ★ ★

BE SOUND IN THE FUNDAMENTALS

The world is full of complexity, and complexity is the enemy of success. We know that in the fog of war, complexity kills. When you step onto a two-way shooting range, whether on the ground or in the air, you will revert to muscle memory. As a result, a hallmark of Joint Force success is that we keep everything simple.

SLOW DOWN

S EALS keep things simple through a fierce focus on fundamentals. No one exemplifies that fierce focus more than the greatest American I've ever known, my SEAL Platoon Chief, whom we will call "Steve."

"Steve" taught me more about the Trident and leadership than anyone else on this planet. A six-foot-four, 230-pound African American with fifty-inch shoulders, you better believe you'd notice this behemoth when he enters the room. As a child, Steve told his grandma he was going to be a SEAL one day. At the time, he couldn't even swim! Still, Steve went on to become one of the most decorated frogs you'll ever meet.

Yet, he's no meathead. In fact, he's very deliberate. So exceptionally methodical and meticulous in his approach to tasks that, growing up in Atlanta, a doctor actually diagnosed him as mentally slow. Nothing could be further from the truth; Steve is deliberate because he's learned that it is what is most effective.

My leadership thought process today comes directly from Steve. Distilled, that thought process is simply: *slow down*.

Steve's philosophy came from his realization that SEALS do a two-year training block before we deploy, then never revisit it again. We're certainly never immersed in it again.

That's why it's so crucial we learn it correctly. One of the first training blocks we do is land warfare. It's one of the most critical blocks since it's fundamental to the training in all the other blocks. Amazingly, though, after first refreshing land warfare, we might not touch it again for another eighteen months—when, this time, it's for real and on the battlefield.

You might not be surprised to hear that when SEALs are in a training block, they tend to get a little fancy. These cocky frogs will try to do everything at incredibly high speeds. But, ultimately, that's not going to benefit you in the long run.

When it comes to real-world missions, the only way a SEAL is going to be effective is if he can refer back to and trust his muscle memory. We focus on training deliberately and meticulously *ad nauseum* on those basic standards right from the get-go. Training is like prepping the room for a paint job—once you've buffed and taped the walls, you can almost just slop the paint on.

That's because we are more intense in training than in combat. We SEALs always say, "The more you sweat in peace, the less you bleed in war." I've certainly learned that to be true. When the bullets start flying, you always revert to the basics, not the high-speed/low-drag stuff you learned many months ago.

This training ultimately pays off when something happens, like unexpectedly running into the enemy in the jungle. Then it's time for a change-it-up-in-a-nanosecond quick drill. It's almost like a quarterback calling an audible after the defense presents him with something unexpected.

As a leader, I'm the one who must make that audible out in the field. SEALs travel light, with very few ammunition rounds or other equipment on us. Making quick calls is crucial, but even if you make the wrong call, our boys are so good we can fix it and course-correct on the fly. The thing is, we can easily correct anything because we all have an incredibly strong grounding in the basics.

CHAPTER 10

MASTERY BREEDS CONFIDENCE

Mastery of the basics works for athletes and military professionals alike. Coach John Giannini's La Salle University basketball team had just come off a 2011–2012 season in which they had won a respectable twenty-one games but had yet again missed the NCAA tournament. Heading home from the arena after losing in the first round of the National Invitation Tournament to Minnesota, Coach Giannini called me.

Giannini—who has a doctorate in sports psychology—felt the one thing his team lacked was mental toughness, citing several key games during the season in which teams like Temple University, St. Louis University, and ultimately the University of Minnesota had simply "out-toughed" his Explorers. Heading into the 2012–2013 season, he thought his senior-led team had a chance to be special—so long as they acquired that mental edge. I believe you acquire a mental edge by first mastering fundamentals.

There are 351 teams in NCAA Division I men's basketball. Only sixty-eight of them make the NCAA tournament every year, and only thirty-four of those win a single tournament game. That's less than 10 percent, and unlike the big-budget schools like Duke University, the University of Kentucky, and Syracuse University, La Salle is essentially a mom-and-pop operation. It's always difficult to win in the NCAAs, but what La Salle tries to do each and every year is something extremely difficult. Luckily, SEALs are experts at doing hard things.

I flew to Philadelphia to meet with the team during the preseason. Coach had told me he didn't want a speech and he didn't want any sort of prepared program the players would undoubtedly just tune out. Instead, he simply wanted me to come in and observe some workouts. So I did just that, hanging out in the corner as the team lifted weights, shot around, and scrimmaged. I made them comfortable with me simply by being around them.

During this time, Coach Giannini clued me in to one key senior who was very emotional on the court, which often hurt the team. He was undoubtedly the team's best player, and an NBA prospect, but late in close games he would often selfishly try to overextend himself, completely ignoring his teammates and what Coach Giannini had taught him. I knew that all he and the rest of his teammates needed was to trust in both Coach Giannini's training and in each other's specific abilities. You do that, again, by mastering fundamentals.

SEALs believe in mastering the fundamentals of everything we do. You might actually be stunned to learn how much intellectually challenging work we truly do. Despite what Hell Week may sound like, we're not just a bunch of lunkheads running around doing push-ups in the surf. We are in fact extremely academic, constantly trying to acquire and then master a diverse array of useable knowledge.

We take photo intel courses for picture-taking out in the field. We learn from renowned ice climbers to help our mountaineering abilities. We even study Russian and other foreign languages we might need one day. It is literally a relentless pursuit of knowledge of the fundamental skills needed for success.

Mastery of the fundamentals comes from repetition. With mastery comes a confidence that our team can and will win under any circumstance. This is the one thing I wanted to stress to the La Salle basketball team to help the players gain that mental edge they lacked: always stick to the basics and follow your training. I asked them, "How do you play well late in a tight game?" You do that by simply relying on your training and each other.

Likewise, Coach Giannini suddenly became far less threatened by the external threats his opponents represented. He now knew if his team simply relied on their training, then that external threat wouldn't matter. And, best of all, that star senior quit trying to over-extend himself, now able to rely more on his well-trained teammates.

Not surprisingly, in 2012–2013, La Salle finally made the massive leap from good to great. Where in the previous year they had lost several tight games, this season they were 7–0 in close games, including an over-time win over Villanova and a thrilling 54–53 victory over ninth-ranked Butler on the last play of game. If you missed their amazing March Madness run on television, the 2012–2013 La Salle Explorers made their first NCAA tournament appearance since 1992, though they didn't win a single game in the event. They won three, marking the first time the university had made it to the Sweet Sixteen since 1955.

★ ★ ★ ★ ★

COMPETENCE MATTERS—BE TECHNICALLY AND TACTICALLY PROFICIENT

One of the NFL teams we worked with featured a simple message written on the top of the whiteboard in the defensive team meeting room. It read "Do Your F-ing Job." A simple yet elegant message. The point was well taken. Don't worry about everyone else's job. If you do your job well, the team will succeed.

Many people rise to leadership positions *simply because they were tactically excellent.* This is not necessarily a problem as long as we understand that being great at your job does not automatically make you a great leader, but the opposite is true. You must attain and maintain a degree of tactical and technical excellence to truly succeed as a leader.

CHAPTER 11

TWO IS GREATER THAN NINE

n SEAL math, two is greater than nine. Prior to 9/11, the SEALs advertised nine different mission capabilities, and we never knew what mission we would be called upon to execute. At this point in our history, we were trying to get any job out there, including foreign internal defense, humanitarian assistance, unconventional warfare, combat swimmer, direct action, special reconnaissance, personal recovery, or combat search and rescue. It was a lot to train for.

But one of the things that we did that really separated us from the other special forces post-9/11, and that I think has been the springboard that has made us the premier special operations force in the world, was our admiral came in at the time and said that "nine capabilities is too much to train for." We're going to advertise two and only two capabilities: special reconnaissance, finding our targets, and direct action, finishing those targets.

This shift allowed us to focus our training on just two core mission sets that we could we could really own, and not just own, but dominate. And in the business world, I've seen so many companies that get in trouble because they try to do so many things as opposed to just picking two to three core missions they can own and dominate and really become world-class at. When the SEALs decided to do that, we became super elite at those missions, to the point that nobody else in the world could do what we could. Our missions started where others ended.

CHAPTER 12

THE FIFTH CORPS COMMANDER

Bitburg Air Base in Germany was the hub of NATO air superiority during the height of the Cold War. Every few months, the entire base would conduct four-day flying exercises, which included airfield attacks, simulated nuclear and chemical weapon conditions, and lots of intense flying.

As a young F-15 pilot, my single focus was on being ready. When not flying, we spent long hours studying intelligence reports, updates to the F-15's weaponry, and any other information that could give us an edge in combat. The prospect for air combat in Europe was varsity-level work. If called, our forces would fight greatly outnumbered, close to home, in tight and contested air space. We were under no delusion that our losses would be low.

The wing represented 75 percent of the permanent F-15 presence in Europe and, as a result, was a high visibility unit. Oftentimes, U.S. and foreign dignitaries with delegations would drop in for a visit. These visits interrupted the important work of staying razor-sharp and ready, and the pilots had little time for or interest in such things. To spread out the pain, the wing would rotate the VIP duty among the three squadrons. When it was your turn, in meant more attention to haircuts, uniforms, squadron cleanliness, and a lot of other things that took time away from much more important work, but such was life at Bitburg Air Base in the 1980s.

Adding to this distraction was the need to occasionally give incentive rides in the two-seat F-15D "family model" to select visitors. These rides were a classic "dog and pony show," which meant extra-short haircuts, sharper uniforms, and more benign flying missions. Extra preparation was required to put on a good show, and since the best you could do was break even, few pilots looked forward to these "opportunities to excel."

As luck would have it, on August 13, 1986, our squadron was "on duty" for VIP tasking for a visit by some Army three-star general, and I was selected by the squadron commander to give this guy a ride in the F-15. Great. So I went through the ritual of getting a haircut, preparing an elaborate briefing on the capabilities of the F-15, and mentally prepared myself for a ho-hum sortie.

The morning of the flight, I learned that my passenger would be the Fifth Corps Commander and that he had never flow in anything faster than a helicopter. Even better. So I prepared myself for the worst while completing a final review of the weather and other relevant flight information.

At briefing time, I heard the squadron called to attention, so I took my place in the briefing room and got ready for the show. In walked the Fifth Corps commander, a rather large and imposing figure, and I could read the last name on his uniform: POWELL.

He introduced himself as General Colin Powell, and we exchanged pleasantries before starting the briefing. Now what you have to remember is that while General Powell was well known to the higher ranks, an Air Force captain flying F-15s at Bitburg had no earthly idea who he was. I should have figured something was going on when every colonel on base followed us out to the jet for our flight.

Upon arrival at the aircraft, tail number 9009, the crew chief guided my passenger up the ladder and started to strap him in while I completed the walk-around inspection. As I got ready to go up the ladder, the wing commander walked over at brisk pace to give me some last-minute instructions. "Don't make this guy sick. He is going to be somebody someday." "Sure, he will," I thought.

The flight went as briefed, and General Powell was eager to learn about what the F-15 could do. I think this had more to do with what we could do to support his troops in the Fulda Gap than anything else. After we landed, we drove back to the squadron for a quick debrief.

It was customary to conduct a quick recap of the mission, then turn the debrief over to the VIP, which is exactly what I did. But unlike other VIP debriefs, General Powell got up out of his chair and walked over the map of Germany we used to brief the mission. He pointed to a spot on the map and identified the Soviet unit by name, type, and commander. He then went into minute detail about each of the military commanders in the Warsaw Pact units across from his Fifth Corps troops.

I was amazed at the level of detail he recited about every single commander of every major enemy unit across the border. He knew where they went to school, what assignments they held, and what higher military education they obtained. To a young captain interested only in flying and fighting, it was an impressive display.

Seeing that a three-star general could be so invested in his current job, rather than his next job, was a great lesson.

General Powell was the master of right now. He was the type of guy I'd go to war with and for in a second, and to this day, I attribute much of his later success in life to his F-15 experience with me.

★ ★ ★ ★ ★

KEY QUESTIONS FOR FOCUS

- What specific goals do you have for your team?
- Do you write your goals down?
- Do you post your goals in prominent places where people can see them on a regular basis?
- Can you identify the strategic outcome tied to each one of your goals?
- Are your goals specific, measurable, achievable, realistic, and time-bound?
- What have you done in the past year to demonstrate you put team above self?
- What specific examples can you cite over the last three months to show you place others above self?
- What are three fundamental skills critical to your team's success?

- What have you done in the last three months to train to these skills?
- How would your direct reports rate your professional competence?
- What have you done in the last three months to improve your professional skills?

★ ★ ★ ★ ★

General Powell lived our leadership model as the Fifth Corps Commander by being the master of right now. He focused on success with specific goals, put team above self, and cared for his troops more than himself. If you follow his lead, you have taken the first steps toward success. Couple that with a solid grounding in the fundamentals while remaining technically and tactically proficient, and you will be well on the path toward our second leadership principle: gaining and maintaining trust—a quality General Powell considers the essence of leadership.

PART TWO

TRUST

Trust is the Glue that Binds Team and Leader

Trust is the glue that binds team and leader. If focus gets your mind in the right place, then trust does the same for your heart. Hard to gain and easy to lose, trust has to emanate and flow from leader to team, and back again. It is the bedrock of high-performing teams and individuals.

As military members, we have taken trust to a whole new level, trusting our very lives to one another. SEALs stand shoulder to shoulder, starting their missions where others have ended, executing complex and dangerous operations where the outcomes are far from assured and the risks are great. Fighter pilots place ultimate trust in their wingman and the dozens of specialists who come together under austere conditions and are involved in maintaining, arming, and fueling our complex machines to ensure they are ever ready for action.

We understand that business is rarely life-or-death. For anyone who has placed their life in the hands of another, whether by choice or circumstances, it is hard to put the feeling into words. We contend, however, that in business and beyond, our economic situation, our relationship with our families, and our spiritual lives are at stake, and that is no less important. To that end, trust plays a key role in the things that matter most, for individuals as well as teams.

In 2012, Google embarked on an initiative to determine which team qualities were most important to team success. Code-named "Project Aristotle" as a nod to the philosopher's famous quote that "the whole is greater than the sum of its parts," the project involved extensive analysis of some 180 Google teams over a period of two years.[4]

---

4   Charles Duhigg, "What Google Learned From Its Quest to Build the Perfect Team," *New York Times Magazine*, Feb. 28, 2016, MM20, https://www.nytimes.com/2016/02/28/magazine/what-google-learned-from-its-quest-to-build-the-perfect-team.html

According to the *New York Times*, the researchers, at first, struggled to find meaningful correlation between team dynamics and success. In the end, however, the answer was loud and clear. Far and away the number-one dynamic most important to team success was trust. Google spent millions of dollars to learn something we will teach you for much less: trust leads to individual and team success.

* * * * *

LEADERS MUST EARN THE TRUST OF THE TEAM

As military officers we are up front with our teams. "I plan to put us in harm's way only when necessary and to bring each and every one of us home." It is the pledge we make before each mission, both in training and in combat. But talk is cheap. We have to walk the walk.

Trust starts with leading from out front. The flight lead is the first one to take off, commit downrange to engage, and shoot. The SEAL platoon leader is the first one off the ramp of the helicopter, into the icy cold water, or through the front door in a breeching action. Under no circumstances would we ask anyone on our team to do something we would not or could not do ourselves, and the same should apply in business.

Earning the trust of the team takes actions, not words. We have worked with leaders who talk a good game but are short on substance, and that seldom turns out well. The actions that speak loudest are selfless, and to that end we found a great example at a children's museum, of all places.

CHAPTER 13

THE CHILDREN'S MUSEUM

Florida's Golisano Children's Museum of Naples (C'mon) is a state-of-the-art facility whose mission is to create an environment where families can play, learn, and dream together. C'mon was the vision of six founders who wanted to create an interactive brain-building play space. Museum construction and operations are 100 percent privately funded by donations and gate revenue, with no government support, and Executive Director Kris Connolly is a dynamic leader who is laser-focused on delivering the mission to the greater Naples community.

Kris will tell you "nonprofit" is an IRS designation, not a business aspiration. As executive director, she has been called upon to make tough choices. When she took the helm, the museum was hemorrhaging cash and needed reorganization. In the face of these challenges, she adopted a simple yet powerful approach to earn the trust of her team.

"Every single decision I make is framed by the same question: what is in the best interest of the museum?" said Kris. "At the end of day, no matter what the outcome, if I made the best decision for the organization, I can put my head down on the pillow at night and rest well." Recently, Kris had the opportunity to put this approach to the test under stressful circumstances.

In late 2017, Naples experienced a direct hit from Hurricane Irma, which wreaked havoc on Southwest Florida. Fortunately, the museum suffered only minor damage, but the storm took a big toll on full- and part-time staff. Between pre-hurricane preparations and post-hurricane cleanup, C'mon was closed for almost two weeks. This meant zero revenue, and it also meant employees went without work or pay.

The leadership challenge came in balancing the financial impact of being closed with the impact on the employees. Since 65 percent of operating revenue is generated by admissions and sales in the café and store, closing for almost two weeks was no small financial event. Kris was faced with a dilemma: should she pay the employees for the time they could not work because of Irma?

At first, this might seem like an easy decision: pay the people. But because C'mon is 100 percent privately funded, the money used for this purpose would have to come from donations and fundraising. Truth be told, most donors are excited to contribute to programmatic elements and exhibits but less enthusiastic about directly supporting operations.

After weighing both sides, Kris determined that paying her people was in the best interest of C'mon. She understood that her people are the reason C'mon is such a special place and wanted them to feel supported under these difficult circumstances. She also understood that her decision would have a huge impact on morale.

This approach, putting the best interests of C'mon ahead of all else, has permeated her team. From visitor experience to personnel actions, fundraising to maintenance, the measuring stick is always the museum. Her team trusts that every decision she makes is in the best interest of the museum, whether they agree with it or not.

And by all accounts, the C'mon team is hitting it out of the park. The museum is debt free, sitting on substantial cash reserves, is the flagship of the community, and hosted its one millionth visitor a full five years ahead of schedule. It is a testament to the dividends that trust can pay, especially when modeled from the top.

CHAPTER 14

SHOULDER TO SHOULDER

So how do you earn the trust of your team? One way is to work shoulder to shoulder. Everything we do from day one in the SEAL teams is designed to build a team, and there's no differentiation other than rank in the composition of that team.

That means that, when training, both the officers and those who have enlisted go through the exact same evolutions together. We live together twenty-four hours a day, seven days a week, doing the exact same thing at the exact same time, with the same expectations placed upon us. If anything, the officers have higher expectations placed upon them because they are required to lead from out front.

We carry this team concept all the way to our uniforms. In fact, the SEALs are the only warfare community in the Navy that wears the exact same warfare designation for officers and enlisted personnel. In surface warfare, for example, the officer's pin is gold and the enlisted pin is silver. The same is true in the submariner community. But SEALs all wear one pin, the gold Trident, which represents the fact that we are one team with one fate. The Trident signifies that we've all come from the same experience and expectations, and we've all come out on the other side successfully.

CHAPTER 15

DECISION TIME

Earning the trust of your team may also require some personal sacrifice, which I learned the hard way at the Air Force Academy. The Academy presented nonstop opportunities for leadership development. At the start of my third year, I was elected to our forty-member class council. The council served as our student government, which meant we elected class officers. As a new council rep, I had a few ideas about how to make the group more effective and, after sharing these with a few of my classmates, was elected class president.

The council was completely voluntary, and since cadets were always pressed for time, I encouraged but did not insist on 100 percent attendance at our meetings. I figured that since each rep had been elected by their squadron-mates, I would treat them like adults. If they did not want to attend, their squadron would lose out, but I was not going to force the issue.

The problem posed by my decision was that it flew in the face of our training on personal responsibility. The larger problem, however, was it also ran contrary to the guidance I was given by the officer charged with supervising our class council.

The officer, a lieutenant colonel bomber pilot, insisted that I take attendance at every meeting. No problem. The kicker was that he wanted me to write up the cadets who did not attend with demerits. Big problem.

The demerit system was a way to enforce the rules and regulations we were supposed to live under. You could earn demerits for leaving water in your sink, trash in your trashcan, and a myriad of other minor offenses. The problem came when you amassed too many demerits. You were safe up to forty per semester. After forty, each two earned you a one-hour "tour."

Tours were performed in full-service dress, with your rifle, hat, and gloves, and required you to march around in a square. They were served after class and on the weekends, and, well, gave you time to think.

"I want you to write up every class rep that fails to show up for the next council meeting for ten demerits and two restrictions," said the lieutenant colonel. "No sir, I won't do that," I replied. "Mr. Demarest, you will write them up, or I will write you up. Dismissed!" Decision time.

I went back to my room and thought about the threat. I already had twenty demerits, so there was not much room to maneuver. "What kind of leader would I be if I abandoned my principles?" I thought. The decision was easy. I was not going to write them up. I told no one of my predicament and scheduled our next council meeting.

Sure enough, five of the forty class reps did not attend the meeting. I took attendance, ran the meeting, and reported to the good colonel the next day. "Mr. Demarest, how many reps missed the meeting last night?" he asked. "Five, sir," I replied. "Are you going to write them up for ten and two?" He knew the answer but waited for me to tell him, "No, sir." "Very well, Mr. Demarest, then I will write you up for each rep who missed," and handed me fifty demerits and ten restrictions. Ouch. Quick math told me I was over by thirty, so fifteen tours.

I left and told no one. I had faith in my classmates and a firm belief in my stance. Their time was more important than mine, and I was determined to prove it, so at the next scheduled tour period, I got dressed up and headed for the tour pad.

My roommate asked, "Where are you going all dressed up?" But as soon as I reached for my rifle, he knew. "What did you get written up for?" "The First Group AOC (Air Officer Commanding) wrote me up for fifty and ten." "Fifty and ten, wow." After he pressed me a bit, I told him my story and hustled out for the tour formation.

Over the following months, I had plenty of time to think, and not once did I regret my decision. Word of my plight spread throughout the council, and we had 100 percent attendance after that, and I never once mentioned it.

My struggles with the First Group Air Officer Commanding lived on. As graduation approached, he made his move. Historically, the senior class president was retained as permanent class president. My pal decided to break with the tradition and called for an election, so the entire class voted. As a result, I am pleased to report that one title that holds a special place in my heart is "permanent president of the United States Air Force Academy Class of 1982."

★ ★ ★ ★ ★

LEADERS TRUST THEIR TEAMS

Nothing is more frustrating than responsibility without authority. We have worked with countless teams who complain they are micromanaged or so closely supervised they are afraid to make a decision. It paralyzes the team and kills initiative. It also drives away good people. Leaders demonstrate trust in their teams when they delegate authority and responsibility to the lowest possible level. Free your people to do the work you hired them for and let them run with it. You will be amazed by the results.

CHAPTER 16

WET DESIGN

WET, or WET Design, makes products you know but is a company you've probably never heard of. Its products are really sensory experiences that combine water, music, choreography, and some serious engineering into a watery art form. Perhaps WET's most famous water feature is the Fountains of Bellagio in Las Vegas. Its purpose, according to CEO Mark Fuller, is "about seeing people enchanted. I like making people feel more glad to be alive."

Mark founded the company in 1983 and still runs it today. He launched with the idea that the laminar flow characteristics of water, which he wrote about in his master's thesis, could be put to use creating water features to enhance the human experience. And to accomplish this, he assembled a team as diverse as they come, including mechanical engineers, musicians, project managers, dancers, graphic designers, choreographers, machinists, and special effects experts, to name just a few. Mark's vision was to blend these skills together into a dynamic team capable of starting with a simple idea they could transform into a massive, robotic water feature that could be installed and maintained anywhere in the world.

While building his team, he had to build a massive infrastructure. State-of-the-art computer design and modeling spaces, experimentation tanks, wood and metal shops, and automated manufacturing to build nozzles, lights, and electrical components that all had to work in and around water. Also, water testing and treatment labs, theatrical lighting design and manufacturing facilities, and space for his team to work, live, and grow.

As WET grew and enjoyed more and more success, Mark continued to pour money into the company. He could almost never say no to a request for the newest toy or technology needed by someone on his team. This approach, of course, did not sit well with his internal financial team. Mark believed in a completely flat organization. As he walked from the computer design areas or through the shops and workspaces, he would constantly stop to check in with his people. And if they needed something, they would print out a work order and ask him to sign it, on the spot. And oftentimes

Mark would sign, leaving it up to the finance team to figure out how to pay for it. Mark demonstrated tremendous trust in everyone at WET and was repaid with an incredibly dedicated and loyal team. The team adapted to Mark's style and adopted his vision as their own, learning how to run a flat organization while delivering awe-inspiring water features around the world, all while making money.

Mark never saw WET as simply a business. Mark saw WET as the vehicle to deliver on his vision, and he has never let go of that. Even as the company has weathered the ups and downs of the global economy over the years, growing and shrinking as the work has flowed in and out, Mark's bank account has not been the sole measure of his riches. Mark is rich in knowing that his work has improved the human condition and will continue to do so, and that WET's success has been built on the trust he places in his team.

CHAPTER 17

MISSION PLANNING

SEALs use mission planning as a tool to build trust in our teams. We don't depend on one person, the leader, to come up with a plan. We use planning cells, which are based on areas of responsibility and experience.

We don't throw a group of SEALs together and expect to immediately operate at peak efficiency. We have to build into that high level of performance by identifying small, defined tasks, giving clear guidance on what the task is, creating a timeline for reporting back progress, and maintaining a single point of accountability for delivering the result.

For example, the point man is always responsible planning our routes in and out of the target area. He determines how to get in to the target, and out safely. And while the team leader has the overall responsibility for every aspect of the plan, it is simply too much work for one person. So the point man starts planning, and we meet for periodic assessments to track progress, give course corrections and guidance, and ensure we are on path to accomplish our specified goal.

When the team first forms, we check in often, but with time, I learn about my team and they learn about me as a leader. They learn what I am looking for and why. And over time, those check-ins become less frequent, and we get to the point where we don't even have to monitor the planning process because by working together over countless hours, in missions and training exercises, everyone knows exactly what is expected of them.

It is a painstaking process that takes a lot of heavy lifting up front, but it allows us to develop trust in simple things, which will pay huge dividends down the road when time runs short and tensions run high.

CHAPTER 18

WING WEAPONS

My career as a young first-assignment fighter pilot at Bitburg Air Base in Germany got off to a good start. I was assigned to my first fighter squadron, the 53rd "NATO Tigers," and loved everything about being a Tiger. After completing Mission Qualification Training, I was given the call sign "Boots."

Our squadron was a tight-knit group of warriors focused only on being the best F-15 squadron we could be. All my friends were in the Tigers, and we had great leadership from top to bottom. I worked long hours and flew as much as I could to earn the respect of my fellow Tigers.

Early on, I was identified as a pilot with potential, so I got upgraded to two-ship flight lead in minimum time. Soon after came my four-ship flight lead checkout, and things were really moving. When not flying, I was assigned to the coveted weapons shop, where my nonflying responsibilities centered on "go to war" training and study. I could not have dreamt of a better start.

My early career goal was to get selected to attend the Air Force Fighter Weapons Instructor Course (FWIC), also known as "Weapons School" and more commonly known as "Top Gun." The nomination to attend Weapons School was ultracompetitive, and the wing could only nominate one pilot for each of the three courses taught per year.

I made no secret about the fact that I wanted to attend Weapons School, and my squadron leadership all knew it. From the Squadron Commander to the Operations Officer to my Flight Commander and our Weapons Officer, they all knew what I was after. And I thought they were all on my side. That is, until I got called into the Squadron Commander's office one afternoon.

"Boots, you are moving to the Wing Weapons Shop to be the Wing Electronic Combat Pilot," said my commander. "You start tomorrow. Good luck." I walked out of that office in a daze. "How could this happen?" I thought to myself. "Wing Weapons?"

The Wing Electronic Combat Pilot (ECP) job had never been a path to Weapons School. And while I had the requisite training as a squadron ECP, I was absolutely not ready to get kicked out of the nest so soon. Wing Weapons was in the headquarters building, which, while only a mile from the squadron, seemed like the other side of Germany. I packed up my desk and was not a happy camper.

So I showed up at Wing Weapons and traded in my gold Tiger scarf for the white scarf of a wing staffer. It was the ultimate disgrace, and I could hardly hide my disappointment. Moving from the constant activity of a fighter squadron to a small office down the road took me away from the action. "Out of sight, out of mind," I thought. Luckily, my training as a military officer kicked in, and I picked myself up, unpacked at my new desk, and got to work.

To add insult to injury, the wing ECP job was a mess. We did not have a coherent electronic combat program, our training plan was outdated, and our pilots did not know enough about the electronic threats and our capabilities to counter them. I jumped in with both feet and got to work.

I was still attached to the Tigers for flying purposes, so I spent some time in the squadron. But when flying was over, it was back to the wing. After a few months on the new job, it dawned on me that my squadron leadership indeed had a plan for me after all.

Leadership knew that what I really needed was exposure to the wing leadership. These were the people who selected pilots for FWIC. They also knew that the wing ECP job was broken, and they had faith that I would put the time and energy in to fix it, and that my efforts would get noticed. Once it dawned on me that all I needed to do was trust the squadron leadership team, I was off to the races.

In the months ahead, not only would I resurrect the wing ECP job, but I was given other high-profile projects that impacted the entire wing. Suddenly the white scarf didn't seem so bad, although I could never quite get used to wearing it.

After placing my trust firmly in my squadron leadership team, I was rewarded with selection to FWIC. Truth be told, I probably got to Weapons School faster than I would have had I stayed in the squadron. To this day, I am one of the youngest pilots ever to graduate from the F-15 Fighter Weapons Instructor Course, and I have my squadron leadership to thank for that honor.

★ ★ ★ ★ ★

TEAM MEMBERS MUST TRUST EACH OTHER

Effective teams contain members who trust each other to get the job done. By definition, a team is a collection of people who need the efforts of others on their team to succeed.

We need people to deliver what they promised by the deadline they agreed to. Since most plans rely on interconnected and sequenced work-streams for success, we must have faith that our teammates will deliver. When they do, trust is reinforced. When they fail, trust erodes. As leaders, we are constantly looking to build trust between team members.

CHAPTER 19

NEWS AT THE NINTH HOLE

After leaving my active-duty SEAL experience it was time to get a "real" job, and in 2002, I got hired as a medical sales representative for Genzyme Biosurgery. I knew nothing about the industry and had to go through another Hell Week to acclimate to the job. Initially I struggled mightily in the corporate world. After years of rubber duck drops and traipsing through foreign jungles, a desk job was a bit boring and unchallenging.

I usually worked alone and out of my home with no bosses watching over me. Those days of medical device sales were the "Wild West." I was allowed to do what I wanted, when I wanted, where I wanted, so long as it was within my geographical territory and I delivered results. In time, my results got noticed and I was placed in charge of a small sales team.

One goal was to hire new sales reps, and as luck would have it, a great opportunity fell right into my lap. Mike was a phenomenal sales rep from Oklahoma City who quickly was becoming such a big name in our industry that he couldn't help but get job offers thrown at him left and right. I immediately realized that would be the case, so I always communicated to Mike, "You will get plenty of great job offers, and other companies are going to come after you. And I'm okay with that." By showing Mike I cared more about him than the company, trust between us began to grow.

Still, I'm not completely sure he fully trusted what I was saying because talk is cheap. In fact, he probably assumed I was just feeding him the old company line. That is, he did until one day when we were playing the golf course right by his house. It was at the ninth-hole turn—as they joke, "bad news always happens on the ninth"—when Mike mentioned he had just received a pretty significant job offer. Out of respect, he had come to me first, still not sure what to do about it.

I told him I greatly appreciated him telling me and, even more importantly, I would gladly help him in his decision-making process to figure out what was best for both him and his family. I let him know I couldn't care less how his leaving might hurt me or our team—I only cared about his happiness and future success.

Suffice it to say, not only did Mike turn down that job offer, but he stayed with me and our sales team for the rest of my sales career. Because of our conversations, he now knew I was that rare boss he could always communicate with freely and, most importantly, that I was a man he could fully trust. It's no surprise Mike has now ascended to a position in the medical device industry far above where I ever was. I'm thrilled for him.

CHAPTER 20

AERIAL REFUELING

Aerial refueling is an unnatural act that seems like the brainchild of two drunks at a bar. Imagine they've been drinking all night and solving all the world's problems. "You know, we need our fighters to fly for hours and hours without landing." "Why don't we just load them will fuel tanks?" "Too heavy, and not enough room for weapons."

"I have the perfect solution. Let's first take an airliner and make it a flying gas station. We'll paint it dark gray, hang a gas hose off the back end, and make someone inside lie on their stomachs and fly the gas hose around with a joystick."

"Nah, gas hoses are for sissies. I can do better than that. Instead of a gas hose, let's use a pipe instead. And

74

let's add a refueling port to the fighter a few feet from the pilot's head, so that the pilot will have to fly in just the right spot." "We can put a set of lights on the belly of the airliner to signal the pilot because we don't want them to actually talk back and forth."

"Yeah, so we'll have them fly real close together, stick the metal pipe in the receptacle, then pump gasoline from one to another. And to make it more sporting, we'll make them refuel in bad weather and at night." "Sounds fun, right?" "I'll drink to that!"

The fact is, the story is not far from the truth. Fighters and tanker join up five miles above the surface of the earth at 450 miles an hour to pass highly flammable liquid down a metal pipe to an aircraft whose engines run at over 1,600 degrees Fahrenheit. No joke. To orchestrate this routine but dangerous dance requires trust between pilot and crew.

The boom operator, also known as the "boomer," has to trust the pilot to position their fighter in the small refueling window and, once connected, keep steady in the window. If the pilot moves outside the limit of the boom envelope, the boom can malfunction, or worse, break off in flight. Bad news for tanker and worse news for fighter.

The pilot has to trust the boomer. Once in position, the boom is literally flown to an exact spot directly in front of the refueling receptacle. In the F-15, this is located on the left shoulder of the aircraft, which the pilot cannot see without using a set of mirrors in the cockpit.

As the probe flies by the cockpit, it passes just twelve to eighteen inches from the canopy and looks much closer than that. And did I mention that the boomers are junior airmen, most of whom enlisted in the Air Force as teenagers? It is a stunning display of trust between two people who have never met.

★ ★ ★ ★ ★

TRUST IN YOURSELF

Character matters. Having trust in yourself means that you've internalized moral and ethical standards and will stand up for them regardless of price or cost. It's about doing what's right when nobody's watching, or when everybody's watching and nobody else stands up.

CHAPTER 21

STAND UP

Each year during my medical device career, all the region's top sales reps were invited to a gala event at a fancy hotel. You know the drill: put on your best suit, hit an open bar, and get a catered meal. But the event also was to feature top speakers, including one of my company's best sales representatives at the time. This was a huge opportunity for Genzyme, and even more so for the chosen sales representative, as she would be speaking in front of dozens of the country's top surgeons, who were also in attendance.

Speeches in the medical device industry are rarely interesting. Government regulations force everyone to follow standardized rules about what can and cannot be said. Essentially, the speaker has to offer full transparency and disclosures as to what a particular drug is FDA-approved for. You can thus imagine my surprise when, during our representative's speech, she went off-script and mentioned that an invasive-surgery product could now easily be tweaked for noninvasive procedures. Problem.

I immediately stood up, like some character in a movie, and called out to the surgeons in attendance: "Ladies and gentlemen, that is a non-FDA-approved usage for this product. Y'all make choices every day about how you use products, and I think you should know that's an unapproved use."

You see, a big trend in the medical world was adversely affecting Genzyme around that time. In the mid-2000s, invasive procedures began drastically decreasing. Unfortunately, you couldn't use one of our top-selling products—essentially a piece of disintegrating wax paper you literally put into the body—in minimally and noninvasive procedures. So how could you still sell this thing?

As an aside, physicians are allowed to prescribe drugs any way they see fit, but pharmaceutical companies are prohibited from marketing them for any use except those approved by the FDA. Still, some clever guys at our company figured out doctors could just crush up each five-by-six-inch sheet of wax paper, turn it into a gel, and then inject that into the patient noninvasively. This was clearly an off-label use (meaning one not currently approved by the FDA) and completely illegal.[5]

Nevertheless, we had guys flaunting governmental regulations and making millions marketing this product's off-label usage, and then selling it to doctors for that very reason. Sadly, many people in my company were turning a blind eye to the laws, something that can often happen in the corporate world when big bucks are involved. I refused.

These were fineable, go-to-jail type crimes, and our leaders were completely ignoring them! Around this same time, Merck pretty much had to shut their doors after the FDA fined the company nearly one billion dollars for their illegal, off-label marketing of the arthritis drug Vioxx.

I wish I had a dime for every time a surgeon of that era asked me the same question they were surely asking my fellow sales reps: "How do I use this product in a noninvasive procedure?" Just like them, if I simply answered the question, I could have made millions of dollars. Instead, and even if it was tough to watch my

---

5   "Genzyme Corporation to Pay $32.5 Million to Resolve Criminal Liability Relating to Seprafilm," U.S. Department of Justice Office of Public Affairs press release 15-1085, Sept. 3, 2015, https://www.justice.gov/opa/pr/genzyme-corpo-ration-pay-325-million-resolve-criminal-liability-relating-se-prafilm

fellow reps raking it in, I did the right thing and refused to ever sell off-label.

I maintained the belief in myself and my team that we could be successful by behaving ethically and legally, even when faced with all these challenges. Sure, some of my employees were angered at how strict I was, but you better believe something like this builds trust in your team and your leadership.

Whether you're a leader in the military, a boss in the corporate world, or a coach for a sports team, you have to play by the rules. You don't need to cheat to succeed, and you don't need to lie to get ahead in this world. Stay true to what you believe in and the results will follow, as there is never a wrong time to do the right thing.

CHAPTER 22

THE HONOR CODE

ntegrity is always doing the right thing regardless of cost and is the foundation of trust. Our service academies each have a simple honor code: "We will not lie, cheat, steal, or tolerate those who do." The first part is easy. It's black and white. No lying, stealing, or cheating. Period. Easy enough. But the second part, known as the non-toleration clause, poses an entirely different problem. If you become aware of an honor violation and fail to report it, you have now violated the code and are subject to an honor board and dismissal. Tough stuff.

My friend Chuck was the model cadet. Super smart, super sharp, and super difficult to go to dinner with. Chuck thought he should get exactly what he paid for. It was a bit embarrassing to watch him send back a steak that looked perfectly fine to me because it was not cooked exactly as he ordered.

He also made a point to go over every single item on the dinner check, and whenever he found a mistake of any kind, he would summon the server. The first time he called a server over about the check, I wanted to shrink into my seat and disappear. "Here it comes," I thought. But to my surprise, the conversation did not go at all as I expected.

"You left off one soda and a dessert," he said and politely asked the server to add them in. I was dumbfounded. I'd never seen this done before. Perhaps my experiences were with great waiters who never missed anything. Perhaps I simply didn't pay enough attention. Whatever the reason, Chuck's approach made such an impact on me that I've adopted it as my own. And while Chuck displayed the kind of integrity worthy of celebration to this day, little did we both know that he would later be put to a much bigger test with life-altering implications.

While Chuck was a model cadet, he had a bit of a wild side to him, and wild sides don't always work within the confines of cadet life. As a result, Chuck sometimes got in trouble—nothing major, but enough that he earned demerits and restrictions. Restrictions are a "confined to quarters"-type of punishment. Once given restrictions, they were served on Friday night and weekends. As part of the process, cadets serving restrictions were required to sign in every few hours. Failure to sign in was a violation of your restriction, subjecting you to further punishment, which was usually more restrictions.

Being young, bold, and aggressive, Chuck liked to push the envelope even when serving restrictions. So one Saturday night, while serving restrictions, Chuck decided to take a quick trip into town to a party before taps. The problem was, it was a long way to town, and Chuck got behind the power curve.

There was no way to make it back before taps. He would miss the sign-in and had to accept the fact that more restrictions were in his future. When he got back, he did not check the sign-in log, figuring the damage was done. He just went back to his room and went to bed.

Chuck spent Sunday dreading a visit investigating why he had not signed in, and worrying about admitting that he was, technically, AWOL. But nothing happened Sunday. It was not until Tuesday that he got a visit informing him that he was reported for an honor code violation about signing in Saturday night.

At first, he had no idea why this was an honor code issue. He thought it had something to do with leaving base, and knew he was guilty of that. But an honor violation? The next day, a key fact came to light when the first-degree (senior) cadet who lived next door told him that he had signed Chuck in to try to keep him out of trouble. That, of course, was a lie, and it put Chuck in a real bind.

When confronted, Chuck did what he always did. He told the truth. No, he did not sign the log, and yes, he knew who did. For some that might have been hard, almost impossible, to do. Not Chuck. But now that an honor violation had been identified, Chuck was faced with an honor board.

The honor system is completely run by cadets. The board had a cadet chair, a panel of cadets to decide the outcome, and cadet witnesses. There are three possible outcomes for an honor board. The first is not guilty, and a cadet found not guilty is immediately reinstated into the cadet wing. The second is guilty, no discretion, which results in immediate expulsion from the Academy. The third is guilty with discretion. Discretion is a prerogative of the honor board to recommend retention of a cadet found guilty of an honor violation because of special circumstances surrounding the case.

The honor board went on as planned. Chuck's testimony was simple. He did not sign his name to the last entry in the log, he knew who did, and he refused to give up the name of the cadet. Some may have been tempted to give up the name of the offending cadet. Chuck saw this as ratting out someone who was trying to do a fellow cadet a favor, and although the cadet was misguided, he did not deserve to get kicked out of the Academy over it. Under heavy pressure from the honor board, Chuck held fast, and the panel went out for deliberations on Chuck's fate at the Academy.

The board came back with its finding—guilty of an honor violation, but a recommendation for discretion. I was relieved. Chuck stuck to his guns, did the right thing in his mind, and kept his character intact. It was a great result, but my elation would be short-lived.

The honor board put in motion a series of events that led Chuck to voluntarily leave the Academy after his second year. I was crushed when he told me the news. How could Chuck, a great student, role model, and pilot, be gone? The Air Force was losing someone who would have made a fantastic officer, fighter pilot, and leader. It simply did not sit right with me.

While many of us were incredibly disappointed, Chuck seemed completely at peace. When I looked at him, I did not see a person fazed; instead I saw someone simply who simply stood up tall and moved on. And then it struck me. Chuck had stayed true to the things he believed in. Loyalty, integrity, and the honor system. He could hold his head high because he had demonstrated the character that made him so special, and to this day, I have never seen someone do something so brave in my entire life. I would trust Chuck with all I have.

CHAPTER 23

THE EAST TIMOR SEA

My dad always told me that, coming into this world, all a man has is his word. People will take you at that word until you give them a reason not to. Your word is your bond, and my bond got tested when promotion time came for my platoon in 1999.

A job in the U.S. Navy is not called a rank, it's called a "rate." A gunner's mate, a rigger, a yeoman, these are all official Navy rates. Back in my day, there were hundreds of different and unique Navy rates—except "SEAL." SEAL was not a rate yet, so they promoted and advanced the Special Warfare community based on typical Navy rate tests.

So let's say you have a guy like me. In official documents I'm listed as Boatswain's Mate 3 (BM3) Mark

McGinnis, when in reality, of course, I'm a SEAL. But in order for me to get promoted and advanced to BM2, I need to receive a passing score on the boatswain's mate test. Yes, I'm tested on my knowledge of a job I've never had before and probably never will have. My future position and income depend on passing this test, yet the Navy is testing me on a rate I don't work in every day.

As you can imagine, not only was the rate test a thorn in our sides and extremely challenging, but most SEALs found it downright unfair. Even worse, these tests were given on exactly one day a year under high scrutiny, with proctors in large classrooms at major Naval bases.

Around this time back in 1999, East Timor was blowing up. Anti-independence Indonesian militants were committing civil atrocities against oppressed East Timorese citizens that were so horrendous we still don't even speak of them. The United States needed the SEALs to immediately deploy there to offer our assistance.

My team was sent from San Diego to Brisbane, Australia, under very low profile, placing one of our landing helicopter assault (LHA) ships in the Timor Sea near Darwin. The plan was for an international peacekeeping force to stabilize the environment and ensure security. United Nations Peacekeeping forces and Australian Special Forces were picked to lead the mission and enter the hostile island environment of

East Timor using SEAL helicopters. We would stay behind on the USS *Belleau Wood* both to offer backup support, and as a "lily pad" for helicopter landings.

Unfortunately, as the "ready" team, this accelerated our timeline, and we were going to miss that one exam date. That happens occasionally, and when it does, you seek permission to hand-carry your tests to wherever you are, administer them yourselves, then mail them back home.

At the time, as a first-time team leader for Juliet Platoon, sitting on our LHA ship in the middle of the sea, I would literally be the only senior Navy officer for thousands of miles. I had an immense responsibility, with nine guys up for promotion and one of them, Rob, at risk of "high tenure." Meaning, if he didn't pass this year's rate exam, his Navy career was done. Even worse, due to his randomly assigned rate, Rob had to take the electrician's test, far and away the Navy's hardest.

You might think there was only one route I could have taken: discreetly giving my men open-book exams. No one would have known, and, in fact, even some SEAL higher-ups back home hinted I probably should do just that. None of my SEAL brethren would have seen this as cheating; most would have simply thought of this as righting a wrong. Giving a good deal to a good SEAL, as we say.

I was under a lot of pressure from all sides while, don't forget, we were in Australia actually trying to become combat capable for a dangerous mission. You'd have thought the Navy would realize our training was more crucial than taking some stupid exams. It was quite a dilemma, and everyone assumed I would be lax and just let my boys take open-book exams. Instead, I staunchly refused. In my opinion, there was only one choice a leader could make.

I devoted our entire days to grueling combat-readiness exercises, aggressively training and rehearsing for our upcoming entry into East Timor. At night, I made my men follow an even more aggressive exam-tutoring program. And, when it came time to take those tests at the end of our deployment, we did it the right way, legitimately with proctors.

The aftermath: all nine guys netted the highest scores they had ever earned on the rate exam, including Rob, who absolutely destroyed that tricky electrician's test. Furthermore, all nine guys got promoted, and, even better, all nine guys reenlisted, even though several were at the end of their obligated active-duty time and could have left the Navy.

This marked the first and only time in Navy history there had been 100 percent promotion and 100 percent retention of eligible SEALs within a platoon. Of course, I wasn't the least bit surprised when I got a call from the X.O. (executive officer, number-two guy) at Naval Support Activity Mid-South (the Navy's admin/ HR headquarters) in Millington, Tennessee. He was, of course, questioning my team's stellar exam scores. We had hand-carried the tests to Australia and then, with no one monitoring us, had blown these tests out of the water? It sounded fishy.

Still, when he told me they were going to do a formal investigation, I wasn't concerned. I simply told him: "No problem." Believe me, this could have been a big-time brouhaha. If I had been found to have cheated, or to have allowed my guys to cheat, my career would have been over. A team of investigators flew to Australia and interviewed us all. Not surprisingly, because of how strictly I had set things up, at the end of the day, all the investigators agreed there was clearly no wrongdoing.

The lessons I learned from this experience have carried forward with me beyond my military career. If I had cheated and allowed my men to take open-book tests, I would have instantly compromised my integrity. If I had compromised that integrity, if I had broken my word, I would have never gotten it back. As a leader, I would have never been able to recover from that mistake, and I would have lost my men.

You see, if I had allowed my men to cheat with an open-book exam, they would have soon begun to wonder: "If he can break the rules for something like this, what else is he willing to break rules for? What would he be willing to do in combat?"

That would lead to even bigger questions of trust. "Would he really lead us home? Is he really invested in us? Does he really care about me more than he cares about himself?"

Instead, I did the right thing, even though senior leadership seemingly wasn't "watching." Don't get me wrong, a few of my men were pissed that I was wasting their time by not letting them just have an open-book exam. Even the Aussie soldiers aboard the *Belleau Wood* were shocked at my strict behavior. "You're making them take a freaking test, mate?"

In the end, giving a good deal to a good SEAL meant demonstrating to my platoon that I had the fortitude to make the tough decisions when needed. They could trust me when their careers were at stake, and that trust would carry over to the battlefield. I had demonstrated a principle that is timeless for leadership: character matters.

★ ★ ★ ★ ★

TRUST IN THE PROCESS

A lot of moving parts must come together to complete most missions, civilian and military. Navigating a twisted and ever-changing path requires processes and procedures to simplify the challenges presented. You don't have to be a "process person" to appreciate the fact that some processes make your team more efficient or effective.

In our world, we use and evolve processes and standard operating procedures to give us greater flexibility during execution. To some, it sounds counterintuitive, but in our experience, creating a framework for action from which we will deviate as circumstances dictate is key. But for this to work in high-threat, high-stakes environments, we have to trust in the process.

CHAPTER 24

LET'S TALK ABOUT THAT SHOT

The University of Houston men's golf team is one of the most decorated programs in NCAA history. The Cougars have won sixteen national championships, countless conference titles, and have sent players like Fred Couples and Steve Elkington to the PGA Tour. But they fell on hard times during the last decade and became stuck in a rut. By the fall of 2009, when the twenty-nine-year-old Jonathan Dismuke was hired as their newest head coach, the once-proud program had plunged to a ranking of 170th in the nation.

Through a mutual connection, I found myself playing a round of eighteen with Jonathan at Houston's Redstone Golf Club early in 2010. I'm a huge golf nut and try to get out on my home course in Austin as often as I can, so I had plenty to discuss with Jonathan.

As we played our round, he spoke openly about his first few months on the job and the severe issues he unfortunately discovered that had pervaded the program since the Cougars were last relevant, in the late 1990s. The key issue, he believed, was that his players were unwilling to take responsibility for overall team development. I told him this all comes down to trust and communication.

Golf would seem to be utterly unique to the other stories discussed in this book. Unlike SEAL teams or corporate units or football and basketball programs, golf is typically seen as a completely individualistic endeavor. Just a person, their club, and a little round ball, right?

College golf is slightly different because of team tournaments, rankings, and year-end championships, but players still have to hit their own shots. It would thus seem like leadership would be totally irrelevant to this one field. That was exactly the problem I saw with that generation of Houston golfers: each player was strictly out there for himself, and it clearly wasn't working.

Though there's obviously a completely different level of intensity, I actually saw plenty of parallels between the SEALs and a college golf team. A sharp mental focus is incredibly important, that fierce focus on fundamentals and creating muscle memory is an absolute necessity, and, most importantly, both need a code of conduct where each team member not only fully shares accountability but is willing to constantly debrief their fellow golfer.

College golf can be quite frustrating for certain individuals on the team. Golf teams will typically have ten to twelve players who practice every single day, but only the five best players are ultimately allowed to participate in tournaments. Depending on the depth of the team, this often creates very difficult situations where a coach is forced to leave very solid players at home. This is amazingly similar to the SEAL teams.

Forty-four SEALs trained for the Osama bin Laden mission, but only twenty-two were sent to the Middle East and ultimately allowed on the ground. Whether in the SEALs or college golf, the challenge for a leader is how to keep those not allowed onto the battlefield, or onto the golf course, in a positive frame of mind. How to keep the overall *esprit de corps* at high levels. You do this by making certain each person feels a part of the team via frequent communication and debriefs.

When I was finally brought in for a practice session, I told Houston's golfers that, much like our SEAL teams, they needed to begin debriefing each other more often and more sharply.

Every day, each person needed to be carefully watching their fellow teammates practicing and playing, and then needed to tell them what they did right and what they could do better. And, each person, no matter how good they were, needed to be open and willing to take these debriefings on their own game. That's the only way you can improve, as both an individual and an overall unit.

One of Coach Dismuke's mottos is, "You can learn lessons expensively or learn them inexpensively." By communicating openly and by frequently engaging in adult conversations with each other, his players began to recognize all of their flaws and what needed to be improved most while in practice. This is how you learn lessons inexpensively, and it leads to fewer mistakes out on the course when the stakes become "expensive" and truly matter.

Perhaps surprisingly, good golfers tend to have good leadership skills. Although not often surrounded by other people, they do have a high level of responsibility. Playing golf is a lot like being a quarterback or a pitcher or even a SEAL commander—you have to have a certain amount of awareness of what is going on all around you. One of the things that good golfers need to do really well is to allow themselves to be held fully accountable for their actions and decision-making.

Company leaders are held to the same tough standards. There's often no one there to bail you out, and that's why you have to be all in all the time, maintaining that game plan, that intensity, and those crucial thought processes. Golf relates well to that—and that's probably one of the reasons all U.S. presidents seem to have an affinity for the game.

The Houston golf team seemed to realize my point and soon began relishing the debriefs. They quickly changed from a team of rugged and introverted individuals to extroverted teammates always looking for chances to communicate with each other, from the twelfth-ranked golfer on the team all the way up to Coach Dismuke.

In 2013, Houston won their first Conference USA title in over a decade. From a ranking of 170th just three years prior, they began the 2014 season ranked seventeenth in the country. They've become a major player in the world of NCAA golf, and a lot of buzz again surrounds the program. Houston seems poised to continue their wonderful legacy well into the next decade, and they have the debrief to thank for propelling them back into contention.

CHAPTER 25

OCEAN CROSSING

n the late 1980s, Europe was the hub of American overseas fighter activity. The Cold War was raging, and in addition to the more than 850 U.S. aircraft stationed in Europe, stateside fighter units routinely rotated into the European theater on training deployments. Such was the case when I arrived at Holloman Air Force Base in New Mexico in 1989, where I joined the Eighth Tactical Fighter Squadron, known as the "Black Sheep."

When I arrived at Holloman, I had already graduated from the United States Air Force's Fighter Weapons School, more commonly known as "Top Gun." I was assigned as the weapons and tactics officer for the Black Sheep. In that role, it was my job to help prepare our squadron for deployments. In the summer of 1990, our squadron was tasked to deploy to Gilze-Rijen Air Base in the Netherlands. Part of that deployment would involve an Atlantic Ocean crossing.

Transatlantic crossings were a regular event yet never routine. We had a detailed process that we followed to the letter. For stateside deployments to Europe, it meant taking off in the middle of the night and flying east for several hours in darkness. The crossing would require a series of aerial refuelings because, at times during the flight, we would be more than twelve hundred miles from the nearest runway, which meant that we had to have enough internal fuel to divert if a malfunction developed.

Aerial refueling is a normal part of fighter operations that seems abnormal to the casual observer. We would rendezvous with a KC-10 tanker, essentially a converted wide-body airliner configured with an aerial refueling probe. The probe, manually operated, used the series of signal lights on the bottom of the aircraft to help the fighter pilot align the air-refueling receptacle with the tanker. Once in position, the boom operator would extend the boom into the receptacle, making contact, and begin pumping fuel into the fighter.

On this particular mission, I was designated as the number three of our four-ship formation. The lead was our squadron operations officer, an experienced F-15 pilot who, like me, had made several previous ocean crossings. As the number-three aircraft, I was also the deputy flight lead, meaning that if something happened to our flight lead, I would assume responsibility for the entire flight for the duration of the crossing.

In all my previous ocean crossings, there had never been an incident where the lead aircraft was forced to return prior to completing the mission. Given my level of experience, the least experienced wingman was assigned to fly with me in the number-four position of the flight of six.

Start, taxi, and takeoff went as planned, and we executed full-afterburner takeoffs at approximately 10:30 p.m. local time, which is an impressive sight if you've never seen fifty thousand pounds of thrust generated by two forty-foot plumes of fire accompanied by thunderous noise. For this particular deployment, the KC-10 departed with us, carrying spare parts and maintenance personnel along for our deployment.

The weather forecast en route was generally good but included the possibility of thunderstorms over the central United States, which were anticipated to cause some weather deviations along the way as we navigated toward the East Coast. So around midnight, as scheduled, we moved from the wing of the tanker into the refueling position to each get a small, two-thousand-pound offload to ensure that our refueling systems were fully operational.

To be honest, I had not paid too much attention during the briefing, having done several ocean crossings in the past and, in this case, not being the primary flight lead. As luck would have it, when our number-one aircraft went to refuel, he was unable to take fuel. He backed out into the pre-contact position, reset the refueling system, and tried again. Once again, no luck. After another try, he made the radio call that changed my night and almost changed my life. He said, "Lead is RTB [returning to base]. Number Three, you have the lead on the left." And with that, he gently turned his F-15 west and headed back to New Mexico.

If there was any chance that I was getting a bit sleepy, that feeling was now completely gone. Suddenly, I was in charge of the five-ship of F-15s headed eastbound in the middle of the night. And when I looked out over the horizon, I began to see lightning flashes as far north and south as I could see. It looked to me as though we were headed directly into some really bad weather, which was not good news at all.

Approaching the storms, as briefed, I radioed for numbers five and six to drop into two-mile radar-trail formation. Our remaining three ships would fly in close formation on the tanker.

Close formation, also known as fingertip formation, is a basic fighter pilot skill that, like refueling, seems to defy common sense. In a fingertip formation, the wingman moves into a position slightly behind the leader and maintains a three-foot wingtip clearance. Yes, just three feet separates the leader and wingman. Because we fly so close, the wingman is forced to spend more than 95 percent of their time staring at the leader to maintain position. Close formation flying requires a lot of concentration and small control inputs, and as a result, it gets old pretty fast.

I proceeded to the tanker's left wing while the number-two aircraft proceeded to the tanker's right wing. My wingman, our most inexperienced lieutenant, in case you forgot that part, moved up to my left wing. That put me smack-dab between the gigantic KC-10 tanker and our newest pilot, with three feet of safe clearance on each side.

For the next ninety minutes, we flew in a fingertip formation through some of the darkest and roughest clouds I'd ever seen. Oftentimes the only thing I could see was the green light on the end of the tanker's wingtip, which was waving up and down in the turbulent darkness.

I couldn't see the tanker's fuselage or anything else on the tanker, including lights. Glued to the moving wingtip light, I could not help but think that, just to my left, flying with only a three-foot wingtip clearance, was our youngest lieutenant. "Welcome to the big leagues," I thought. It was the longest ninety minutes of my life.

As the sun came up, the weather broke, and I could feel the tension flow out of my hands and feet as we moved back to a more comfortable flying position for the crossing. The rest of the flight went as briefed, and we landed in the Netherlands without incident. As I taxied in, I felt a rush of relief. After the aircraft was chocked, I shut the engines down, opened the canopy, and took a deep breath. I then gathered my equipment and made my way down the ladder. For the first and only time in my military flying career, I got down on my hands and knees and gently kissed the ground.

CHAPTER 26

PACKING A PARACHUTE

Trusting in the process is a daily event because the SEAL teams are maniacally committed to process and procedure. In the business world, so many companies that we work with, when we talk about process and procedure, make an X with two fingers. "That's voodoo. That's black magic," they say. "We want to stay away from it at all costs." But in reality, it is critically important to make sure you are set on a pathway toward success rather than spinning out of control with no chance of accomplishing your objective.

Here is a simple example: packing a parachute. We have a very simple riggers checklist for packing a parachute. I can give it to a Master Chief with thirty years of experience and five thousand free-fall parachute jumps. He takes out that checklist, which he is required to do, every single time he packs his parachute. In addition, he's required to get a certified expert at packing parachutes to sign off on each checklist item. This process ensures that, even though the Master Chief has made thousands of jumps and packed countless chutes, in his haste to get the job done, he won't forget a critical step that could cause a malfunction.

I can then take that same checklist and give it to a newly minted ensign who's brand-new to the SEAL teams on his first free-fall jump, and even though he's unfamiliar with the process and task, he won't forget any of the critical steps either. So what I've done, in effect, is level set experience across twenty-nine years. That way, everyone is on the same page and pointed in the same direction by simply packing a parachute with the same checklist. Our trust in the process ensures safety and mission accomplishment.

★ ★ ★ ★ ★

KEY QUESTIONS FOR TRUST

- What have you done in the last six months to earn the trust of your team?

- When was the last time you worked shoulder to shoulder with a direct report to complete key work?
- What have you done in the last three months to protect your team from adversity?
- When is the last time you planned a project alongside your team?
- What are three examples where you delegated authority and responsibility to your team for a key outcome?
- How do you react when a top performer moves on to a better opportunity?
- What actions demonstrate that your team members trust each other?
- What recent example would you use to demonstrate you do the right thing when nobody is watching?
- Who is the person you admire most, and why?
- When was the last time you stood up against the crowd or authority over something you believe in?
- What key processes do you have in place to ensure team success?
- When is the last time you updated your key processes?

- How do you monitor the effectiveness of your key processes?
- What processes get in the way of success?

* * * * *

Whether crossing the ocean or packing a parachute, trust is the glue binding team and leader. Leaders must start by earning the trust of their teams every day, then demonstrate through actions that they have trust in their teams. Team members must trust each other to enjoy success as a group, and they must possess the character to trust in themselves. Combine all of that with trust in the process, and you will be ready to fold in our third leadership principle: communication.

PART THREE

COMMUNICATION

*The Art of Communication is
the Language of Leadership*[6]

—James C. Humes

The most common mistake people make about communication is assuming communication has occurred. Leaders must be the source of constant, clear information and guidance, communicated both horizontally and vertically. Without a relentless commitment to information sharing, a team is doomed to mediocrity at best.

---

6   James C. Humes, quotation on leadership, posted March 27, 2008, https://www.freshbusinessthinking.com/the-art-of-communication-is-the-language-of-leadership/

Done well, communication becomes the lifeblood of success and can fuel a team through good times and bad. Our experience in both military service and business is that those who embrace the task as a journey and not simply a destination stand the best chance of sustained excellence, and like most things, it starts and ends at the top.

★ ★ ★ ★ ★

COMMANDER'S INTENT DRIVES A CONSTANT MESSAGE WITH VARIED MESSAGING

Teams need a roadmap to success. They require clear, measurable goals with specific deliverables by a certain date. The messaging must vary while the message remains steady. What teams need, first and foremost, is to understand their leader's intent and make it their own—something we in the Navy refer to as "Commander's Intent."

CHAPTER 27

COMMANDER'S INTENT

There's no bigger communication tool than clearly laying out the Commander's Intent. In my opinion, it is the single most powerful leadership tool we have as Navy SEALs. Specifying a Commander's Intent means that, as a leader, I tell you the "what" and you have to figure out the "how." In other words, I tell you what I want accomplished, and then you figure out how it's going to get done. When I employ Commander's Intent, I've taken my plan and turned it into our plan, which is crucial for building ownership, focus, and trust.

Intent is based on purpose, not objective. When I give someone a task, I attempt to paint a very clear picture of my desired "end state." I tell them, "When this mission is finished, this is what I want to have happened, and this is what I want that to ultimately look like." Then I simply walk away and leave it up to them to figure out how to get to that end state. The team has to fill in the blanks, figuring out all the tasking steps—the who, what, when, where, and why—from start to finish. Talk about empowering.

Commander's Intent allows for both flexibility and autonomy while still working inside our team framework. Of course, this can sometimes be scary, especially to followers not quite up to the challenge. These are people who simply want to punch in, be bossed around and micromanaged all day, then collect their paycheck at the end of the week. SEALs don't do that. We all want to be empowered and allowed to take charge of our destinies. That's why we're all leaders to a certain extent.

As SEAL Commander, I eventually began asking each man to rewrite our mission statements for me, just so I knew that he understood it. After that, it was strictly up to him. I initially only used Commander's Intent for the overall mission. Then I began to take it a step further and started making my men utilize it for all five phases of a mission: Insertion, Infiltration, Actions on the Objective, Exfiltration, and, finally, Extraction. This became immensely helpful and greatly improved my men's "Go/No Go" analyses as well as their decisions in the heat of battle.

Even better, it made it much easier for us all to figure out those hard-to-detect short-range goals that would eventually lead to the long-range successes we all desired. If you don't plan out your short-range goals, then how can you ever accomplish the long-range objectives? Ultimately, Commander's Intent really changed how the SEAL teams did business, in terms of both performance and success. All team members were capable of taking control of a situation, seizing the initiative, and ultimately grew as leaders themselves.

CHAPTER 28

MERIDIAN GOLD, PART TWO

Early in *Joint Force Leadership*, you were introduced to Meridian Gold, a midsize gold producing company formerly headquartered in Reno, Nevada. Meridian created a strategic plan that was reduced to a simple picture of a mountain. On the slopes were the major milestones, and at the summit was a flag bearing a number representing the future production goal of one million ounces of gold a year. The rest of the story is about how Meridian used their mountain as a communication tool.

Earlier you learned that Meridian's mountain was posted everywhere, which was a good start. In the break room in Reno, the control room of their major mining operation in Chile, and any place they did business. But it was more than a poster campaign; it was their Commander's Intent.

Meridian's leaders knew constant communication of the million-ounce goal was crucial, so they worked hard to fold it into the fabric of the company. Aside from the picture in the conference room, I first noticed the mountain in Meridian's PowerPoint template. The company logo was still there, but the mountain occupied the other corner. "Nice touch," I thought.

Next, I noticed that most leadership meetings began with a trip back to the mountain. Sometimes it was just the title slide in the deck, while other times it was the first topic of discussion. Things were no different out in the field. I saw the same application and approach in the Atacama Desert in northern Chile as I did in the office in Santiago.

The mountain served as a rallying point for office and field operators alike, and it was not a flavor of the month. In the eighteen months or so I spent at Meridian, the mountain was never far away. The goal of one million ounces a year was consistently messaged and delivered through a variety of means so that the entire organization could rally around a clear goal. And they were committed to the million-ounce mark right up until the day the company was acquired at a handsome price.[7]

---

7 Laura Mandaro, "Meridian agrees to Yamana's $3.5 billion merger bid," (see chapter 3, note 1)

CHAPTER 29

PAINT A PICTURE

Pilots are simple creatures, just ask any SEAL. We are trained to search out data from a variety of sources, while moving at the speed of sound, and distill it all down to usable, actionable information. At combat speeds, a threat pointing at us forty miles away merges with us in 120 seconds or less, so time is not on our side.

We battle the speed and complexity of operating in a three-dimensional environment where people are shooting at you from all angles with simplicity. One of the ways we overcome complexity and facilitate communication is through varied messaging of a simple message. To us, varied messaging means using a host of different mediums to send and receive the information needed to succeed.

Our message, or Commander's Intent, is the mission for today: "Gain and maintain air superiority over a SEAL platoon conducting a hostage rescue mission for thirty minutes starting at 1053 Zulu time." The mission means denying enemy aircraft access to the airspace within twenty miles of our friendly force by destroying them or chasing them away. It's a simple mission that we must now convert into action.

Our messaging starts as we prepare to brief our missions. The briefing rooms contain several whiteboards, maps, and visual aids mounted on clear plastic sliding panels. The flight lead creates an elaborate visual presentation, listing an overview of the mission, specific objectives, and detailed drawings of weapons envelopes and tactics. We use different colors to organize the boards by topic and subtopic and also build a lineup card, which is a 4x6 card each pilot will carry that contains critical flight information, such as radio frequencies, timing details, and air-refueling data.

A few minutes before brief time, flight members enter the briefing room and fill out their lineup card. The briefing starts with a time hack to synchronize every watch to the exact second, and the flight lead conducts the briefing. We use the visuals to conduct an oral presentation of the mission, yet another medium. We will reference the maps and draw pictures of our planned tactics and responses. We wrap up with any questions and then prepare to step to the aircraft.

Prior to stepping, we take a few minutes to "chair fly" the mission. Alone, we each review what we just heard, think about what our roles and responsibilities are, and visualize the mission. We find a quiet place and think through each phase of the mission, going over exactly what we are going to accomplish. It is a lot like stretching before exercising, as it gets us ready for action.

We step to the jets, conduct our preflight inspections, and then up the ladder we go to strap in. Once strapped in, we are waiting to crank engines at the exact start time briefed. If we are within visual range of each other, the flight lead will use a hand signal for engine start. So yes, we use hand signals on the ground, as well as in the air.

Once airborne, we continue with hand signals, then transition to relying more on electronic means as we spread out the formation. Using both secure and nonsecure radios, we use a series of pre-briefed code words to convey critical actions and information during flight. While fighting, we will also use the digital displays for our radar, weapons system, and defensive systems. Most importantly, we use a digital display for data fused from a variety of sources to create a three-dimensional depiction of the battle space.

By using written products, pictures, maps, words, hand signals, and digital displays, we vary the messaging while staying focused on our mission of protecting those guys on the ground from air attack. It is an absolute requirement to make sure everyone is on the same page, no matter how they best process information. Besides, pictures and small words are not just the stuff of SEALs.

★ ★ ★ ★ ★

CADENCE AND CANDOR ARE THE HALLMARKS OF GREAT COMMUNICATION

Communication is not a fire-and-forget event. It is a disciplined and sustained effort to share key information with those who need to know. If you think communication has been fully accomplished the moment you hit "send" or when dashing off an email, you are fooling only yourself. Effective communication requires a regular rhythm and honesty that we call cadence and candor.

Cadence is the frequency of your efforts. How often are we going to meet? Should we have regular calls to check in, and if so, how often? Will we rely on email or newsletter updates? And while there is no one answer, if we plan out the timing of our information exchanges, there is a much better chance that our cadence will foster, not hinder, our communication goals.

Candor is about truth and honesty delivered without malice or ill intent. Early in life we are taught to tell the truth, right up until that time when we learn that truth has degrees. "Don't lie, but if you hate what grandma serves for dinner, tell her you like it and eat it."

Effective teams live for candor. Give it to me straight so that I can learn from it or do something about it. Don't sugarcoat it. SEALs and fighter pilots alike insist upon respectful truth over artificial harmony. In fact, if you ever saw us at work after each mission, you might think we didn't like each other because we are brutally honest in evaluating our performances and calling ourselves and each other out when needed.

We've found that the most effective teams gravitate toward candor over worrying about hurting people's feelings. Don't get us wrong, the goal is not to attack people or their efforts. But if we understand up front that the entire team benefits from candor, then people understand that critical comments are not meant personally. They are simply a faster way to get to the point so that we can learn and move on.

There is no better illustration of this point than our SEAL and fighter pilot post-mission debriefings.

CHAPTER 30

THE DEBRIEFING

n my opinion, what takes SEALs from a good special operations unit to an elite special operations unit is a critical step after the mission is over. We can plan a mission with the best of them with exact details, we can cascade that plan to the team through the briefing, and we can then go out and execute that plan at a high level. And most companies in business can do this as well. But we insert another step that makes us elite, helps us identify shortfalls and gaps, and prevents us from making the same mistakes more than once. We debrief after every evolution, training, or combat situation, and we learn to debrief from day one in BUD/S.

Post mission, we gather in a room and check our egos at the door. Debriefing is only about getting better.

Only team members who participated in the mission are invited to the debrief, which is run by what we call a "pipe hitter." The pipe hitter is a senior member from an experience perspective, regardless of rank, who has authority derived from respect and influence, and whose job is to keep everybody in check.

We start by reviewing what we said we were going to do, then comparing that to what happened. We then ask, "What did we do right, and what could we do better?"

We try to conduct the debrief without emotion. We avoid finger-pointing and blame because it's all about simply identifying issues we need to fix or identifying and celebrating our successes. We then take those lessons learned and cascade them throughout the organization to make everybody better. The key is to incorporate what we learned from this mission into the next plan so that we (and others in the organization) don't repeat the same mistakes next time.

CHAPTER 31

MORE DEBRIEFING

Fighter pilot debriefs mirror the goals of a SEAL debrief, with an added level of detail. Far and away, debriefing is the secret sauce of fighter aviation. Our average training sortie lasts about an hour, and of that hour, fifteen to twenty minutes is actually spent training. The rest of our time is spent getting to and from the airspace and setting up to fight.

It costs hundreds of man-hours and tens of thousands of dollars an hour to fly and maintain these sophisticated machines, and as stewards of our nation's resources, we have a responsibility to make the absolute most of our training time. So after we land and put away our life-support equipment, we gather together to debrief.

Before the formal debrief begins, we each take time to review our tapes. Each aircraft is equipped with a video recording system that captures our heads-up display, radar display, and audio. We take notes on the significant events from each engagement, and then we gather together for the formal debrief.

The debrief starts on time, and the flight lead begins by restating the objectives we set for the mission. Next, we quickly cover the flight administration, noting and correcting any deviations from the briefed plan. We then settle in to the meat of the mission: each engagement.

One by one, we reconstruct what happened by diagramming each engagement on the whiteboards. We then watch every single pilot's tape, since tapes don't lie, to confirm what each flight member did. We pause at critical moments and assess the validity of every simulated shot taken. We painstakingly dive as deep as required to determine exactly what happened. Only then can we analyze our results.

Analysis is the key to maximizing our training. We identify what went well and capture it for use on our next mission. More importantly, we find every error made, not for the purpose of crushing anyone's ego (which is hard, if not impossible, to do to a fighter pilot), but for the sole purpose of fixing it. To err is human, but to repeat mistakes in my world is a crime.

Mistakes in training can cost lives in combat, so we take the debrief with deadly seriousness.

Our debriefs are so serious that, to the casual observer, it might appear that we don't like each other much. We are brutally honest, and no one is above the debrief, regardless of rank or experience. If the boss flew with us and made a mistake, they are going to hear it from us unfiltered. It may sound harsh, but we all understand that "what's right" is more important than "who's right." The good news is that the boss expects us to treat everyone the same and calls us out if we don't.

Once the debrief is complete, we share our best practices and lessons learned with the entire squadron to accelerate everyone's experience. We don't keep what works and what does not a secret. All too often, when we work with businesses and sales teams, people play the "I've got a secret" game to their personal gain but to the detriment of the team. Not in our world.

If you want to be part of a high-performing team, put aside personal success and replace it with team success. Insert a debrief at the end of every major milestone or event and watch your team soar to new heights.

CHAPTER 32

DEBRIEFING IN ACTION

During the New York Giants 2011 and 2012 seasons, we worked with the team generally and the players specifically on communication cadence and candor. Our goal was to help improve on-field and off-field communication among the players, which is key to successfully executing modern NFL schemes. For this work, we turned to the debrief.

Now most people would think the coaching staff has a lot to do with the players' communication. While this is generally true, it is not entirely the case. In the end, once the players step on the field, it is up to them to organize and effectively communicate key information quickly in a high-speed, dynamic environment.

NFL teams are great at film study. After every game, the position coaches sit down with their players and review performance on every play. Each play is graded and measured against the desired performance for that particular play. Coaches look at where the players lined up, their technique, how they reacted, and, ultimately, the results delivered on the field.

Now you might think this would involve a completely open and honest dialogue between coaches and players, but that is not necessarily always the case. Remember that coaches decide who plays and who does not, and who stays and who does not, and as a result, there is not always 100 percent open and honest communication between players and coaches.

The Giants' 2011 campaign was marked by an up-and-down regular season. When we first started working with them, the team was 4–2 and playing well, but the defensive coordinator, Perry Fewell, insisted that his unit needed to communicate more effectively going forward. Enter us.

Our job was to work directly with the players to improve their communication, and to effectively fill this role, we had to earn their trust. We had to convince them our sole objective was to improve their performance on the field, not to spy on them and report back to the coaching staff.

This was critically important because if we were going to make real progress in improving communication, we had to have very frank and open discussions about what was working well and what was not. Sometimes the problem was with the coaching staff. More often, there was an on-field issue that reduced communication effectiveness.

So we taught the players how to conduct their own debrief. No coaches, no staff, just players. At first, I was not sure if it would work. We got the entire defensive unit into a room and started to "debrief." What was supposed to be an organized session quickly degenerated into a heated shouting match involving perhaps a few four-letter words. While it was not what we had in mind, we would later learn that the players thought it was important to get a number of things off their chests before moving on.

Shouting match aside, we facilitated several "players only" debriefs. They caught on quickly, and soon we were not needed and, in fact, probably not welcome. No problem. We understood that the only people who should attend the debrief are those with skin in the game. Debriefing is not a spectator sport.

We continued to work with the team throughout the year, right up to the playoffs. It was great to see the team come together aided by the debrief. On the field after their victory in Super Bowl XLVI, and while working with the team the following season, players and coaches alike agreed that the cadence and candor created in the "players only" debrief was an important part of their run to the Lombardi Trophy.

CHAPTER 33

SHARE AND
SHARE ALIKE

Gathering and sharing information is the heart of communication, and simplicity matters. If we can answer the "who does what by when, and why?" we stand an excellent chance of success. To that end, here are the questions we ask and answer to build out our communication plan. If you keep these in mind, you will keep your information flow at the right pace and volume.

The first question we ask about an upcoming communication is, "What desired outcome or end result are we looking for?" We look at the end state first to ensure we are driving toward the strategic or tactical goals we've set. "At the completion of this presentation, we want our commander to approve execution of our rescue mission as planned." By keeping the end state in the foreground, we can always answer the question, "Why are we sitting in this meeting?" Often, we work with teams who cannot clearly answer this question. Time is too valuable to waste, however, so it is critical that we make sure we are acting with purpose.

Next we explore the purpose of the communication. Is it to inform? Confirm understanding? Request action? Warn? Document action already taken? Arrive at a specific decision? Whatever the purpose is, we state it up front to ensure people listen for information key to their role. For example: "We are going to brief the highlights of the infiltration, action on target, and exfiltration of our rescue mission in enough detail to enable you, the boss, to make a decision to approve our plan."

Communication should not happen by accident. Our third step is to identify specific triggers. What event or activity triggers the need to share information? Market events? Customer concerns? Regulatory action? Competitor activities? Scheduled reporting? By pre-identifying important events, we minimize the chance of missing something and encourage our teammates to speak up. While we cannot and will not cover every possible trigger, simply having the conversation reminds everyone to seek out and share key information.

Once we find that nugget worth sharing, we ask, "How soon do I need to pass this on?" Timing matters because, at times, information is fleeting and loses value if not immediately shared. Other times, it can wait. To keep things simple, we suggest three categories: immediate reporting, report when able, and save for our regularly scheduled meeting or call.

Now that it's time to share, let's select the most efficient and effective means available. Phone call? Text? E-mail? WebEx? Conference call? A face-to-face meeting? While we will not dwell on the virtues and vices of each, here are a few thoughts: First, there is no substitute for face-to-face communication if we really want to ensure clarity. Body language, facial expressions, and the ability to ask follow-up questions all help minimize errors. Second, if you write them down in some format, there is a better chance that the key elements will not be missed. Finally, use the method best suited for your audience, rather than the one you like best.

Next, who is the originator or organizer, as in, who will initiate the message? Should it be the first person to learn the news? The team leader? The admin assistant? We need to be clear about who starts the effort and spell out whether we must confirm receipt, or if there is any requirement to follow up.

Finally, we need to be clear on the intended audience. Is this a broad message to the entire organization or targeted to a select few? It is important to consider whether there are any legal or compliance issues related to this message, or any confidentiality or disclosure concerns. For emails, let's avoid sending it to the dreaded "all" list whenever possible, since our goal is to balance the need to share information with the need to free up time to work. And remember, we must communicate both horizontally with our team and vertically with other stakeholders and partners.

CHAPTER 34

DELL COMPUTER

Dell Computer provides an excellent example of horizontal and vertical communication across a wide range of audiences.[8] Dell faced a major communication challenge in 2004 when the company embarked on a revolutionary approach in the ultra-price-competitive PC market. With competitors "averaging 50-90 days of finished goods inventory, Dell set the target for its OptiPlex plant at zero!"[9] To ensure this goal was met, the plant had no warehouse, and finished goods were shipped directly off the assembly line.

To keep things really lean, Dell moved its goal for component inventory from several weeks to no more

---

8   J. Stewart Black and Hal B. Gregersen, *It Starts With One* (Upper Saddle River, NJ: Wharton School Publishing, 2007), pp. 122-131.

9   Ibid., 123.

than two hours of inventory. That's right, two hours! Dell's plan was supported by a widespread and sustained vertical and horizontal communication effort.

The horizontal communication component focused on suppliers. Dell had to convince each supplier to support the new vision by clearly articulating the answer to the question "What's in it for me?" Dell started by inviting the suppliers into the Dell system and giving them access to Dell's demand signals in exchange for granting Dell access to their production capacities. By reducing the delivery time for confirmed orders to just seventy-five minutes, suppliers would have to locate inventory close to Dell production facilities.

The tight tolerances, in turn, made Dell heavily dependent on timely deliveries, which made the suppliers a more critical component of the Dell system. This co-dependency created more certainty for the suppliers, which allowed them to reduce completed component inventory and enjoy the resulting working capital and cash flow benefits.

The vertical communication component focused on customers. Since 85 percent of Dell's business came from companies,[10] they focused on the ordering process. At the time, most companies used a manual system requiring several levels of approval prior to

10   Ibid.

ordering, then after the machine was built, it went back to the company's IT department for software loading and testing. The entire process, from employee order to delivery of a work-ready machine, could take two to three months!

Dell developed preapproved computer configurations and created custom online ordering systems to make the buying process smoother. In addition, it fostered relationships with key individuals within each customer's organization who would act as champions for the product, reinforcing the productivity and cost benefits of this new system. Oftentimes, customers would receive fully operational products just three or four days after they were ordered. The sustained communication effort eased the natural resistance to an entrenched process and played an important role in Dell's success and that of their customers and suppliers.

While the Dell example shows the power of horizontal and vertical communication across an expansive front, the same principles apply to communication at a more tactical level.

CHAPTER 35

BUT DON'T
OVERDO IT

The F-15 is equipped with three radios. One is a receiver only tuned to the universal emergency frequency. The other two are fully functioning ultra-high frequency (UHF) radios, called the front and back radios. Their names come from the fact that both are operated from the same multifunction switch on the right side of the right engine throttle. Push forward for the front radio and back for the rear radio. Not too complicated, but three radios can be a lot to listen to at one time.

The back radio is our flight common frequency. Typically, this is used for inter-flight communication within our two-ship or four-ship. Calls on this radio include system checks, ops checks, and flight admin. It represents the horizontal component of our in-flight communication (comm) between team members. Pretty simple, but we use comm brevity and code words to minimize chatter on this radio, freeing us up to listen to the front radio, our primary audio communications link.

The front radio is for communication outside of the flight, which represents the vertical component of our comm system. For ground operations and departure, we are talking to the tower and departure control. En route to the training airspace, we contact the air traffic control center responsible for the area. When we enter the training airspace, we are off to yet another frequency.

During training, we often work with military Ground Control Intercept (GCI) radar facilities or Airborne Warning and Control System (AWACS) controllers, whose job is to help paint the air picture for our missions. It is critical to build situational awareness of the air-to-air and surface-to-air threats to ensure our F-15s can gain and maintain air superiority across the battle space.

Joining us on the common "fight" frequency might be a package of Air Force, Navy, or Marine strike assets, jamming aircraft, and specialized aircraft tasked to seek out and destroy surface-to-air threats. And of course, the frequency is also monitored by the Combined Air Operations Center, meaning the boss can always hear what's going on.

This vertical communication network allows for a real-time exchange of information critical to mission success, but because of the sheer number of potential talkers on the frequency, it requires an ultra-disciplined approach.

Achieving effective communication requires everyone to read and heed a strict comm protocol. First, before anyone keys the mike on the fight frequency, they must ask, "Is this information everyone needs to know?" If the answer is yes, then continue. If the answer is no, or "I'm not sure," then hold off. Indeed, much of our pre-mission planning and briefing is dedicated to the comm plan. Second, we identify who the call is for. Finally, we add directive comm, followed by descriptive comm. For example, when we see that a surface-to-air missile (SAM) has been launched on the aircraft ahead of us, the call might be, "Claw Flight, break left, SAM, left nine o'clock low."

The goal of our plan, or any comm plan for that matter, is to improve situational awareness, not degrade it. Sounds simple, but in the heat of battle, training, or real world, it is much easier said than done. We are constantly training for the real thing because we know that effective communication can be the difference between mission success and failure, in combat as well as in business.

When we practice and achieve comm discipline on both our horizontal and vertical frequencies, we exponentially improve our chances to survive and prevail in the dynamic environments in which we employ. Key in this effort is the need for clear understanding, which is aided by use of a common language.

★ ★ ★ ★ ★

WORK TO BUILD A COMMON LANGUAGE

We live and work in an increasingly diversified world. Our teams are comprised of people with a variety of educational, cultural, and experiential differences. And while this diversity gives us strength, it comes at a cost, and that cost is the lack of a common language. Simply put, we need our words to convey the same meaning to everyone on the team for effective communication to take place. In our experience, there is no better way to overcome this challenge than by working together toward a common goal.

CHAPTER 36

RED FLAG

Nellis Air Force Base in Nevada is home to the world's most comprehensive joint force training exercise, Red Flag. Founded in 1975, Red Flag missions are flown on the Nevada Test and Training Range, which offers more than 15,000 square miles of airspace and 4,700 square miles of restricted land. Since inception, more than 440,000 military personnel from over twenty-eight countries have honed their combat skills at Nellis.[11]

---

11 U.S. Air Force Fact Sheet, 414th Combat Training Squadron "Red Flag," July 6, 2012, https://www.nellis. af.mil/About/Fact Sheets/Display/Article/284176/414th-combat-training-squadron-red-flag/

A typical Red Flag exercise involves a variety of attack, fighter, bomber, reconnaissance, electronic warfare, air superiority, airlift, search and rescue, aerial refueling, and command and control aircraft, plus ground-based command and control, space, and cyber forces. In addition, Special Operations, aircrew recovery, and ground forces routinely take part in the exercise.

Aircraft and personnel deploy to Red Flag to use their diverse capabilities to execute specific missions, such as air interdiction, combat search and rescue, close air support, dynamic targeting, and defensive counter air.

When you combine coalition forces with U.S. Army, Navy, Air Force, and Marine ground and air elements into one exercise, it becomes clear that one of Red Flag's major goals is to improve the interoperability of U.S. and coalition partners, which requires building and training with a common language.

The building process begins during pre-mission planning. Every single participating unit sends a small planning team to the mission planning room, where the overall mission commander sets the training objectives, tactics, communication plan, and timing. Armed with a clear understanding of the Commander's Intent, the group breaks into functional support elements with their own commanders to create a synchronized master plan.

Using the communication plan as a template, each element mission commander further breaks out targets into separate packages and matches each target to the asset most capable of delivering the needed effects, all while setting the code words and providing greater detail on the communications brevity plan.

If the mission includes air insertion of ground forces, the entire mission timing is centered on getting those forces to an exact spot at an exact time supported by a covering force. And from the mission commander to the last jumper off the ramp, everyone is aligned to a common language, regardless of country or unit of origin.

Building a common language requires a sustained effort supported by regular and realistic training in exercises like Red Flag. We've learned that putting smaller teams together and practicing is the only way to stay sharp. The same holds true outside of the military. The best way to build and sustain a common language is to bring our diverse teams together to work on a mutual goal. Done well, it creates greater efficiency, cohesion, and, ultimately, results. Left unattended, our situational awareness fades and, along with it, our likelihood of sustained and predictable success.

RED FLAG

Red Flag and other exercises are excellent tools for building a common language, and we put these skills to the ultimate test out in the real world.

CHAPTER 37

THE 9-LINE

Creating a language shared by soldiers, sailors, airmen, and marines is not as easy as it perhaps sounds. Each military branch has its own history, culture, and customs. Add to that the litany of different acronyms that permeate the military, and what we have is a recipe for miscommunication. Heck, are we using a latrine, bathroom, restroom, head, or toilet?

To make matters even more interesting, when our troops are in contact with the enemy and need air support, we ask them to get on the radio and talk to the pilot about the support they require. Think about that. You're in a foreign country, in the middle of nowhere, with people shooting at you, and we want you to make a radio call for help. What could possibly go wrong?

Our solution was to create a universal communication format called the "9-Line" brief. The 9-Line is used throughout the world by U.S. and coalition partners as the standard format to request close air support or medical evacuation. It does not matter what branch you are in or whose military you serve. The 9-Line is the universal language for air support.

Our common language is rooted in the specific format used. For close air support, a mission where we drop ordnance on targets threatening friendly forces, the 9-Line includes:

1. Initial point
2. Attack heading
3. Distance from initial point to target
4. Target elevation above mean sea level
5. Target description
6. Target location
7. Type of weapon and terminal guidance
8. Location of friendlies
9. Egress direction

Here is what the radio call might sound like: "Rodan Flight, Nine-Line as follows: Intersection of Highways Ten and Seventy-five, three-four-zero degrees, five kilometers, one hundred twenty feet, enemy tanks in the open, GBU-thirty-eight, friendlies two kilometers north, egress west and hold in wheel above target."

So perhaps you are thinking, "I don't think I will ever be in a position to call in an air strike, even if I wanted to, so how does this apply to me?" The answer is that building a common language starts with agreeing on some type of communication rules.

For example, what is the rule for using acronyms? Does everyone on my team know the meaning of every single acronym? If so, use them, but be careful. In our experience, few people will stand up and admit, "I don't know what that means," even if most people are in that boat.

Next, we suggest using a common format when able. How many times have you read an email and had to hunt for what it was asking of you? Try this strategy we've learned over the years for writing an email:

In the subject line, make sure the first word identifies why the email is being sent. "Information," "Action," "Decision needed." This alerts the recipient as to the purpose of the email.

In the body, try BLUF, meaning, "bottom line up front." I want to know your major point first, and the details or explanation can follow. This might seem simple, but when you think about the number of emails you get daily, adding just a little structure can go a long way.

Building a common language takes effort. Up front, establishing a few ground rules will help align your team. Next, take time to make sure people really understand what you expect from them. Ask them to repeat back your instructions to ensure clear communication. Watch out for language barriers. Our diverse workforce is a blessing, but when working with people whose first language is not English, opportunities for errors increase, and those can be, well, embarrassing.

CHAPTER 38

THERE'S ALWAYS ROOM FOR IMPROVEMENT

The Mexican Air Force (in Spanish, *Fuerza Aérea Mexicana,* or FAM) was born in 1913 during the Mexican Revolution.[12] The FAM operates under a national commander, while the second-in-command is the Air Force Chief of Staff, who supervises a Deputy Chief of Operations and a Deputy Chief of Management. The FAM and United States Air Force

---

12 Mexican Air Force, www.globalsecurity.com, https://www.globalsecurity.org/military/world/mexico/air-force.htm

have a long history of cooperation in the form of military exchanges and common equipment.

During the Cold War, the FAM procured the U.S.-built Lockheed T-33 Shooting Star, a subsonic fighter used as a patrol and interceptor aircraft, and, in the early 1980s, it added the Northrop F-5E Tiger II, giving Mexico its first supersonic platform. The FAM also operates a variety of helicopters and transport aircraft.[13]

Military exchanges were common, and by the mid-1980s, the Twelfth Air Force, then located at Bergstrom Air Force Base near Austin, Texas, was managing all military interactions with Mexico. In 1989, the Twelfth Air Force Commander invited the FAM Chief of Staff to visit Bergstrom and offered him a ride in the F-15, the Air Force's premier air superiority fighter. The only problem was that the Mexican general did not speak much English.

To solve this dilemma, the U.S. Air Force scoured its records to find a Spanish-speaking F-15 pilot, which is where I come in. My mother was born and raised in Mexico, and while we did not speak Spanish around the house much while growing up, I had basic conversational skills and a pretty decent Mexican accent. So I got the call and began planning for the big day.

---

13 Ibid.

My preparation started with the realization that I would need to sharpen my conversation skills, especially when it came to describing detailed technical information about a sophisticated aircraft. My Spanish experience up to that point revolved around making small talk with relatives every few years. I had never tried to translate my fighter pilot experience into Spanish.

My mother was all too eager to help. We got on the phone almost every day for a month before the flight, practicing my conversational Spanish. We also spent time literally making up Spanish words. At that time, we could not find a source document to translate "heads-up display" from English to Spanish. My mother asked, "Well, what does it do?" "It's two pieces of glass displaying a computer picture of aircraft performance and weapons data." I replied. "Okay," she said. "We'll call it 'two pieces of glass with a picture.'" And off we went, making up dozens of new words describing the radar display, weapons panel, radar warning receiver, and other core functions of the F-15. It was tiring work, but I was looking forward to the challenge.

After nearly a month of preparation, it was finally time to take a two-seat F-15 to Bergstrom to complete my mission. I flew in the day prior and got a briefing about my passenger. The Chief of Staff of the Mexican Air Force was an experienced pilot, so I was now sure that my preparation would pay off, and that I would be able to show him the full capabilities of the mighty F-15 Eagle. There was one detail that I forgot to ask about, which would later come back to bite me in a big way.

On August 23, 1989, I awoke early and proceeded to the flight briefing area on base. The first order of business was to prepare the briefing room. I had prepared three pages of notes in Spanish and had carefully written out the entire flight profile in my best Spanish. I wanted to make a good impression and planned to demonstrate the entire performance envelope of the F-15 to him.

The general was an impressive man with a distinguished career in the FAM, so I was really looking forward to giving him an F-15 ride. An interpreter accompanied him during the briefing, so if I struggled for any words during the briefing, I had help right there—help I would not have when we got in the airplane. The briefing went as scheduled, and we stepped to the jet on time for our flight.

When we got to the aircraft, the crew chief took the general up the ladder and strapped him into the back seat while I conducted the preflight walk-around. Satisfied that the jet was ready to fly, I climbed the ladder and, with the help of the crew chief, buckled in for the flight. The start and taxi went as planned. As was common practice, my planned profile included a maximum-performance takeoff, so after final checks, we taxied onto the runway for departure.

Now a max-performance takeoff is an impressive event, whether you are inside the aircraft or on the ground watching, and I wanted to give the general a good show. So I selected full afterburner and was airborne fifteen hundred feet down the runway. I sucked up the gear and flaps and held the mighty Eagle on the deck in a full-afterburner acceleration. By the time we got to the end of the runway, we were passing 450 knots, and the max-performance profile called for me to plant the Eagle on its tail and streak skyward to fifteen thousand feet.

As we passed the departure and the runway, I sucked the stick back into my lap and pointed the Eagle toward the heavens, and at that moment heard the loudest cry of *"Ay, Dios Mio!"* (Oh, My God!) I had ever heard. I looked back in the mirrors and saw the general holding on to the canopy rail handles for dear life, and his eyes were as big as saucers. Not thinking much of it at the time, I continued our climb, only to hear the second-loudest *"Ay, Dios Mio!"* when I rolled the Eagle over on its back to level off at fifteen thousand feet.

It was at that moment that I realized I had failed to ask an important question—perhaps the most important question. So, in my best Spanish, I asked,

"General, have you ever flown in a fighter jet before?" And he quickly answered, "No." I was baffled. First, it had never occurred to me that the FAM Chief of Staff could be a cargo pilot and not a fighter pilot. Second, I was professionally embarrassed that I had never asked the most basic question of my guest.

Needless to say, I was forced to abandon most of my ambitious flight profile, and the mission quickly turned into a sightseeing tour of the Texas countryside. We returned to the base, and I was able to gently kiss the runway on our landing. When we got out of the aircraft, the only thing the General could say was, "That was such a smooth landing."

From that experience, I learned the importance of building a common language, and to this day, I have made it my mission not to repeat that mistake ever again.

★ ★ ★ ★ ★

KEY QUESTIONS FOR COMMUNICATION

- Have you developed your Commander's Intent?
- Have you deployed your Commander's Intent to the entire team?

- What is your preferred method of passing key information?
- What methods do your team members prefer for passing key information?
- How often do you have regular calls or meetings with your team?
- What days and times do you make available for calls with team members?
- What would prevent team members from bringing you bad news?
- What tools do you have in place to critically evaluate both wins and losses?
- How do you capture best practices?
- How do you pass along best practices to your team?
- What would you show someone who asked to see a copy of your business communication plan?
- How often do you communicate with your key external stakeholders?
- What do you do to protect your team from information overload?
- How do you build a common understanding of your business with your team members?
- What rules do you have about the use of acronyms?

- What are the biggest communication barriers you face with your team?
- Do you use a specific tool or process to share key information?

★ ★ ★ ★ ★

There is always room to improve your communication, which is essential because the art of communication is the language of leadership. Commander's Intent lets every person on the team know exactly where we are going, and it is delivered with a constant message using every possible medium available. Effective communication requires candor, including those tough grown-up talks, and must happen on a regular basis. Leaders must communicate horizontally and vertically to ensure clear reception. Finally, we must strive the build a common language so that messages are received and understood as they are intended. When you add effective communication to a team with focus and trust, the sky is the limit.

FINAL THOUGHTS

Welcome to the varsity team. If you've heard that before, then you know it comes with responsibility, the chance to work hard every day, and the opportunity to drive your team toward success. If you've not heard it before, now you have!

We have shared with you our perspective that leadership is about uniting people behind a goal worthy of their time and effort, requiring focus, trust, and communication. Why these three pillars? First, our lives are filled with distractions, requiring us to continuously focus and refocus on the task at hand. Second, the only teams that are worth being on are those built upon trust. And finally, effective communication is the linchpin of leadership.

Leadership is a journey, not a destination, and the road is paved with people who failed as leaders because they became complacent. They thought they had "arrived" when they were designated as leaders, only to be left in the dust when they failed to grow. You can avoid this pitfall by emulating the qualities of the most successful leaders you know while staying true to your own style and skills.

Our challenge to you is to keep seeking out feedback and new skills. You should never be satisfied with your leadership skills. If you can embrace the journey, you will remain relevant and worthy of the leadership opportunity placed before you.

Commander Mark McGinnis
United States Navy
SEAL

Colonel Jim "Boots" Demarest
United States Air Force
Fighter Pilot